Here's what experts are saying about *Accountability Leadership!*

"In this most perceptive analysis of accountability, Gerry Kraines builds on the well-known work of Elliott Jaques and takes this essential management concept to a new dimension."

—Francis Carpenter
Secretary General
European Investment Bank

"*Accountability Leadership* is more than a conceptual treatment....It is a practical approach, with great tools, to identify and develop outstanding leaders and to create an organizational structure and processes that promote accountability and performance. It demystifies the notion of leadership with a set of principles that are clear and straightforward to implement."

—Terry de Jonckheere
President, South America Operations
Ford Motor Company

"Dr. Kraines and the teachings of The Levinson Institute have been a continual source of enlightenment to our staff of world-class biotechnologists at Lilly Research Labs."

—Richard DiMarchi
Group Vice President, Lilly Research Laboratories
Eli Lilly and Company

"Delivering world-class results requires world-class leaders and leadership systems. Accountability Leadership breaks through the hype with an approach that is simple, tested, proven, easy to implement, and consistent with common sense. Managers will wonder why they have not been using this approach all along."

—David J. Lesar
Chairman, President & CEO
Halliburton Company

"Dr. Kraines has crystallized his years of teaching and consulting into a useful handbook for new leaders. Accountability Leadership provides a roadmap for establishing a high-performance culture and developing a pipeline of talent. This should be basic reading for all new managers."

—Charles G. Tharp
Executive Vice President, Human Resources
Bristol-Myers Squibb Company

Accountability Leadership

How to Strengthen Productivity through Sound Managerial Leadership

By
Gerald Kraines

CAREER
PRESS

The Career Press, Inc.
Franklin Lakes, NJ

ACCOUNTABILITY LEADERSHIP
EDITED BY JODI L. BRANDON
TYPESET BY JOHN CASALE
Cover design by Johnson Design
Printed in the U.S.A. by Book-mart Press

To order this title, please call toll-free 1-800-CAREER-1 (NJ and Canada: 201-848-0310) to order using VISA or MasterCard, or for further information on books from Career Press.

The Career Press, Inc., 3 Tice Road, PO Box 687,
Franklin Lakes, NJ 07417
www.careerpress.com

Library of Congress Cataloging-in-Publication Data

Kraines, Gerald.
    Accountability leadership : how to strengthen productivity through sound managerial leadership / by Gerald Kraines.
        p. cm.
    Includes index.
    ISBN 1-56414-551-4
    1. Leadership. 2. Executive ability. 3. Organizational effectiveness. 4. Personnel management. I. Title.

HD57.7 ,K725 2001
658.4'092—dc21

2001035876

Dedication

This book is dedicated to my three mentors in the field of leadership:

Samuel H. Kraines, M.D.
Harry Levinson, Ph.D.
Elliott Jaques, M.D., Ph.D.

Acknowledgments

Two people are most directly responsible for my being able to write this book: my wife, Cynsie, who has counseled and encouraged me through long days and nights; and Robert Krock, my VP, Knowledge Management, who has helped me to refine and to make far more accessible the ideas presented.

The inspiration for this book came from my clients, who have taught me in the past two decades as much as I have taught them; and my students, who have taught to me to synthesize, integrate, reformulate, and simplify. Thanks to Francis Petro, Denis Turcotte, John Gibson, Warren Knowlton, Aaron Schacht, Rae Marie Crisel, Mikael Gordon, Joe Ausikaitis, Tony Bhalla, Terry de Jonckheere, and Debbie Zemke—great leaders, clients, and friends whom I would follow into battle any time they ask.

Ken Lizotte and Tom Gorman were of enormous help in helping to develop a logical structure for the book and in finding and working with my wonderful publisher, The Career Press. And very special thanks go to Harry Levinson and Elliott Jaques, both giants in the field of leadership.

Contents

Foreword

You are about to embark on a remarkable journey of exploring the theory and practice of sound, common sense, and accountable leadership. You may struggle with some of the new language and new definitions. You may be uncomfortable with terms such as hierarchy and subordinates. You may have doubts about the science underlying aspects of structure and human potential. But you will begin to build a mental model about an attainable system.

My training has been in science, specifically in organic chemistry and in medicine. What I am describing is nothing less than a total system—in the sense of a human being functioning as a totally integrated and self-contained system.

This book asserts that leaders of any employment organization can fully implement a total managerial leadership system that will release anywhere from two to three times its currently realized potential. It challenges shareholders and boards of directors to ask whether the full potential of their resources is being harnessed and converted into the value they seek from their organizations. My thesis flies in the face of most of the management fads that have swept across the boardrooms and executive suites over the past five decades, fads that leave a confused, dispirited, and disengaged workforce behind.

The book also challenges the employees and managers within every organization to question the assumptions upon which everyday working conditions are based. Is it inevitable that companies will create unreasonable stress and confusion, pitting people against each other? Is it fair for top management to lean on your sense of loyalty and personal responsibility to compensate for organizational dysfunction created by their failure to apply sound leadership practices? Can our families and neighborhoods and cities grow and prosper when places of employment fail to recognize and develop the potential of employees?

It is my hope that you and everyone reading this book will begin to examine carefully the places you work and ask whether you will help to bring back accountability, clarity, fairness, and trust.

—Gerald A. Kraines, M.D.
July 2001

Part I:
Leadership & Accountability

More than 70 percent of U.S. companies' capabilities are untapped and poorly aligned. What a waste, to both shareholders and to the people working within! Leadership is always about leverage, and all managerial systems require accountability leadership. This book shows you what accountability leadership is and how to apply it successfully.

In Part One, we introduce accountability and the concept of LEAD:

- Leverage potential.
- Engage commitment.
- Align judgment.
- Develop capability.

In Part II, we'll explore the power of LEAD and in Parts III and IV, we'll examine its full and practical application.

Chapter 1
The Accountable Organization

Tim Hinkley[1], a participant at one of the Accountable Leadership seminars I recently led, approached me during the Tuesday afternoon break. He is a senior manager in the software division of a company supporting heavy manufacturing industries. Tim had a problem, and his nervous grimace told me it was a bad one.

Tim's department, market-and-systems development, identifies opportunities in the industries his company serves. His group also identifies the requirements—functions, specifications, operating platforms—of software products that can exploit those opportunities. On the same managerial level as Tim is a head of R&D, which is the group where software engineers develop the actual products. There is also a head of sales and service, who brings the products to market and provides support.

Tim told me that the division CEO holds him accountable for developing and delivering software solutions for the sectors the company has targeted. However, the people who develop the software—the engineers in R&D—are not subordinate to Tim. They are instead subordinate to the head of R&D, who, like Tim, is subordinate to the division CEO.

Having heard this much, I found myself nodding in recognition. I had heard this story before. "I depend on the people in R&D," continued Tim, "but I don't have managerial control over them, and it's almost impossible for me to get what I need from them." Tim went on to point out that his department and R&D were driving each other to despair. "My people go to them with software requirements we identify in market surveys and careful on-site discussions with customers. And they think we're hopeless bureaucrats out to stifle their creativity."

Of course, Tim had shared his problem with the division CEO, whose response was, "Fix it!" On several occasions, the CEO had told Tim that it is his job to "deliver" R&D, and that "he's accountable for getting those solutions to market." Moreover, the CEO assured Tim that he totally supported him in his mission. Yet, on several occasions, he also told Tim and the head of R&D that they both "need to work this out between themselves." Meanwhile, the R&D chief feared that he would lose his staff if he tried to hold them accountable. Everyone on his staff, he knew, had numerous employment alternatives.

Given the look on Tim's face, he had not been able to "fix it," nor had the CEO's exhortations of support been of much help. However, Tim pointed out that after participating this far in the seminar, he had recognized his situation clearly for the first time. Tim was mired in a system of managerial abdication, bad hierarchy, and accountability gone awry. This is not to portray Tim as a victim destined for ruin. There are steps he could take to remedy, or at least ameliorate, the situation. But the CEO's managerial approach within the current organizational structure was the main obstacle to Tim's continued good mental health and ultimate success.

Systems Gone Awry

People in employment organizations work within managerial leadership systems and defined structures. Employees and managers apply—or fail to apply—their intelligence, judgment, skills, energy, and creativity within those systems and structures. Therefore, to restore or achieve high functionality, an organization's systems and structures must be put in proper order. And they must be aligned with its strategy.

In a situation like the one in Tim's division, it is not enough for the CEO to exercise charismatic leadership or to empower Tim or to encourage teamwork or to commit to the customer. As attractive as these one-dimensional measures are (and they are attractive in their simplicity and "people-orientation") such approaches typically generate short-term euphoria and set people up for later failure. They are, in fact, simplistic approaches to the requirements of a complex work system.

In Tim's situation we have abdication by the CEO on at least four dimensions of good managerial leadership practice:

1. The CEO failed to define the context within which his subordinates must operate.
2. The CEO failed to hold the head of R&D accountable for his people.
3. The CEO failed to give Tim the authority he needed to achieve the result he had been told he was accountable for achieving.
4. The CEO created a structure in which it is difficult, at best, for market-and-systems development and R&D to work well together.

The CEO's only solution is to become more actively involved in getting Tim and the head of R&D to work together. That's because as it stands, the CEO is, in effect, saying, "Tim, I want you to compensate for my abdication of my leadership accountabilities and for my failure to accurately define accountabilities and authorities properly." That is a task that no subordinate should be asked to take on for his manager.

Does it surprise you to learn that situations similar to Tim's exist in innumerable organizations around the world today?

Accountability You Can Count On

To begin, let's examine the current view of accountability among people working in organizations today. My own informal, but extensive, survey reveals that most people hold a decidedly negative attitude toward accountability. Perhaps that is your attitude as well.

What comes to your mind when you hear the word accountability?

If it's something along the lines of "who gets the blame?" or "being called on the carpet" or "getting set up as the fall guy," then you're like most people.

When I ask business audiences how accountability feels, most people say "uncomfortable" or "painful." When I ask if they would welcome accountability, most say, "No, thank you…at least, not the way it's practiced in my company."

Why has accountability, which is merely a principle of sound managerial practice, gotten such a bad rap?

Senior managers have too often invoked accountability as a way of getting things done that they themselves don't know how to get done in the existing less-than-perfect systems and structures. These managers tell people, "You're accountable!" and expect that somehow things will get done. Sometimes this dubious ploy actually works. After all, when their boss says, "Just get it done!" many people can—though sheer willpower, brute force, and long hours—overcome managerial abdication, systemic dysfunctionality, and structural flaws. But the wear and tear burns people out and suboptimizes the whole.

As a managerial technique, holding people accountable after casually tossing a goal or task to them—without setting the context, securing the necessary resources, and providing the proper structure—is destructive. It generates negative emotions and behaviors. It has also generated the widespread negative response to the proper and requisite notion of accountability.

As a first step in rehabilitating accountability, I give you the following accurate, useful definition of the concept:

Accountability is the obligation of an employee to deliver all elements of the value that he or she is being compensated for delivering, as well as the obligation to deliver on specific output commitments with no surprises.

Obviously, employers themselves are also accountable for delivering certain elements of value (most obviously, compensation and proper working conditions), and we'll look at those as well. For the moment however, let's stay on the employee's side of the desk.

The essence of employee accountability becomes clear by comparing the role of an employee with that of an independent contractor. A contractor is accountable for delivering a measurable, usually quantifiable, product, service, or result. Repair the roof. Install a phone system. Collect past due accounts. In the process, it is the contractor's absolute right to make a profit—ethically, but at your expense—as long as you receive the value you requested. And a contractor is on the hook to deliver the agreed-upon output, no matter what. If a contractor comes back to you and says, "Gee, I figured wrong on my time and materials. Now I can't make a profit," you get to say, "That is too bad, and I am sorry, but we have an agreement and we're sticking with it." The motto for the contractor is *no excuses*. A contractor is left on his own to work within his own process to secure resources, generate efficiencies, and produce results.

Your only concern is the result. The contractor has to figure out for himself how to do it profitably.

An employee, on the other hand, has no right to make a profit at the employer's expense. Instead, an employee is accountable for increasing the employer's profit. The contractor is concerned only with improving his process; the employee cannot just do his job while ignoring other company processes. The employee is accountable for delivering value consistent with the total requirements of his role. In turn, employees do have the right to be compensated at a level consistent with the value they contribute.

Employees are (by law!) paid every day, come what may. They also typically receive training, development, and benefits. Employees expect this of employers.

Like contractors, employees are typically accountable for delivering fixed, measurable, defined results. Increase sales by 15 percent. Hit all production targets and the specified quality standards. Control costs within budget. And like contractors, employees are on the hook to deliver unless they can convince their employer beforehand that it's not going to be possible or desirable to deliver.

The employee's motto must be *no surprises*. If the employer (via the accountable manager) agrees to change the requirements, the employee is now off the hook for the old ones and on the hook for the newly defined ones.

Fixed vs. Relative Accountabilities

The term accountability in a managerial system refers to obligations, some of which are fixed and some of which are relative. Fixed accountabilities comprise the employee's obligations to deliver outputs and to use resources and processes precisely as specified by the employer. **Fixed accountabilities** are necessary to keep processes in control and can be summarized in two distinct categories: commitment and adherence.

- **Commitment**. Employees must fulfill the output commitments exactly, in terms of quantity, quality, and time parameters, as defined in their assignments, projects, services, and other deliverables—unless the manager agrees to adjust them. Under no circumstances can the employee surprise his manager at the due date with changes.
- **Adherence**. Employees must simultaneously observe and work within defined resource constraints—that is, the rules and limits established by policies, procedures, contracts, and other managerial guidelines, as well as by law.

The fixed employee accountabilities—the results, deliverables, rules, and limits associated with a position—are the most obvious and often the only ones managers focus on. However, all employees also have **relative accountabilities**. These have to do with adding the elements of value that are required by the role the employee occupies. Relative accountabilities include the following four catelgories:

- **Reach**. Employees are expected to add as much value as they can in their roles by signing on for ambitious yet achievable targets, rather than hanging back or committing to "low-ball" goals.
- **Fit for purpose**. Employees must continually strive to ensure the optimal means of producing the resulting output, in order to support the purpose for which it was assigned.
- **Stewardship**. Employees must manage company funds and other resources efficiently (as though they personally owned them) exercising additional stewardship by seeking ways to continually improve and conserve those resources, wherever possible.
- **Teamwork**. Employees must recognize that it is the concerted effort from and between everyone to contribute fully to an optimized process that generates profit in an organization, rather than isolated individual efforts to maximize personal output. Therefore, an employee must, at all times, adjust to accommodate other people's work across the organization to maximize the total organizational value—even if her job becomes more difficult.

Many managers do a poor job of defining, explaining, and gaining commitment to fixed accountabilities with their subordinates and holding them to those commitments. Even more fail to properly explain relative accountabilities (if indeed those managers are aware of them by any name) and to accurately assess their subordinates' effectiveness in delivering on them.

There are, as you know, managers who over-budget expenses so they'll look good next year. There are salespeople who sell customers more than they need, just so they'll reach their sales quota this year. There are operating personnel who overpay for materials because it's easier than shopping around. All of them, and employees like them, are failing to fulfill their relative accountabilities. Clearly articulated relative accountabilities—those that every employee has relative to the rest of the company and to the requirements of her own role—are the antidote to the pursuit of narrow goals, waste of resources, and lack of team play that renders so many employees, and their companies, ineffective.

A word of caution: Improper use of incentive pay often diminishes employees' focus on relative accountabilities. Pay-for-performance often amounts to a bribe. It subtly changes the employer-employee relationship by shifting the employee's attention from improving the company's profitability to improving his own. As a result, potentially valuable employees become hybrid subcontractors who direct their energy toward playing the system rather than optimizing its results.

So we see that far from being about blame and reprisals and childish fears of "getting caught," accountability should focus on the very adult matters of expectations, obligations, commitments, and adding value. This is not far from the sentiment that the English historian Thomas Carlyle first expressed in 1843: "A fair day's wages for a fair day's work."

QQT/R = A Crystal-Clear Assignment

The alphabetic expression QQT/R, developed by management scientist Elliott Jaques,[2] represents a small but powerful tool for clarifying fixed accountabilities. It is the simplest way for managers to accurately define an assignment delegated to their subordinates.

In QQT/R:

Q_1=Quantity

Q_2=Quality

T=Time

R=Resources

Note that the slash in QQT/R does not indicate arithmetic division. It merely divides the employees' output accountabilities (quantity, quality and timeframe) from their resource/process accountabilities (constraints and boundary conditions within which they must operate).

Managers have two types of accountabilities: those of every employee and those unique to the managerial role. Chief among managerial accountabilities is to be clear with their subordinates about what (the quantity and quality of output) they are expected to deliver and about the time they have to deliver it. Managers are also accountable for describing and providing the resources required by employees in order to deliver on their assignments.

In virtually any environment, when I ask employees how clear their managers are with them about *what* they are accountable for getting done, most will say, "Not very." Even in manufacturing, QQT/R is not used rigorously enough. For instance, a supervisor may specify an increase in quantity but not the acceptable reduction, if any, in quality. Yet the very basis of lean manufacturing, statistical process control, and just-in-time working requires unambiguous clarity about accountabilities and the interaction between quantity, quality, time, and resources.

Many managers assume their subordinates know what they are accountable for. However, these managers do not realize the tension and anxiety they inadvertently cause by failing to be clear. Typically, a highly responsible subordinate will make his best guess at reading the boss's mind, hoping to be in the right ballpark. Then, a few months later when the manager receives a progress report, the manager will say, "That's not at all what I wanted." This causes unnecessary frustration, wasted energy, and distrust. Some managers even persist in a practice I call "managing by finding the rocks." These managers put their people through an ongoing game of 20 questions and, as a result, develop a gun-shy team made up of fearful individuals who are unwilling to take even the smallest risk.

On the other hand, QQT/R creates unequivocal clarity regarding obligations. Specifically, the formula puts all four variables on the table so managers and subordinates can examine, discuss, adjust, and commit to each one explicitly. The elements of QQT/R are independent, but also *interdependent* variables that sum up real-world constraints and possibilities. There are both possible and necessary trade-offs among them. (Such a trade-off is expressed less formally in the workman's question: "Do you want it done fast, or do you want it done right?")

With the trade-offs on the table, managers and their subordinates are positioned for a hard-hitting, objective conversation about the manager's goals and resources and about the employee's ability to meet those goals given the available resources. When this process is ignored or done haphazardly, employees are saddled with their managers' unrealistic or unfair expectations, and managers delude themselves with their employees' acquiescent or deceptive commitments. When management extracts so-called stretch commitments from employees that are obviously unobtainable, or when it under-resources an effort, employees know what's happening, and feel they've been taken. Similarly, when employees won't commit to challenging goals, they are sabotaging their managers and their company.

Some managers fear that tools such as QQT/R inhibit initiative and creativity. QQT/R does just the opposite. Both initiative and creativity lay in the employees figuring out *how* best to deliver on their commitments—not in deciding *what* they are to deliver. The best employees delight in improving processes and conserving resources while hitting their QQT objectives. The definition of QQT/R should not be construed as top-down either. It should be the outcome of active, vigorous, two-way discussion between managers and their subordinates about the most ambitious yet realistic way the subordinate can support the manager in achieving his QQT/Rs.

Other managers initially believe that QQT/R cannot be applied to people in analytical or research positions or other areas of knowledge work. Our clients involved in R&D, product, technology, or market development, and similar functions don't use QQT/R to define results, per se, as much as they do to mutually define the processes, steps and resources that must be developed, which, in turn, should yield the intended results.

Here, a senior vice president of R&D gives an assignment to her subordinate, a vice president of new technology development.

Given that our long-range plan calls for bringing our third-generation products to market by 2010, I need for you to develop or acquire new technologies that will support their effective design by 2008. You will need to work with the vice president of business development over the next two years to characterize:

- The types of technologies, both the science and applications.
- The centers currently engaged in research about them.
- Other companies that we could license technologies from, acquire, or create a joint venture with.

In addition, you will need to identify the types of skill sets and level of people we will need to recruit, hire, and develop over the next five years in order to have a team capable of converting those core technologies into practical-application vehicles.

As is true for all accountabilities, QQT/R is not meant to be a straightjacket or a rigid set of rules. Rather, it is a useful tool for managers and employees to use in developing clearly articulated, mutually agreed-upon commitments. It is the most efficient means of ensuring that the output delivered to the manager is really the output he wanted. Significantly, QQT/R captures some of the managers' accountabilities as well as those of employees by defining the resources the manager commits to deliver. Yet, as powerful as QQTR is, it still does not capture all managerial accountabilities.

What's a Manager to Do?

Managerial accountabilities can be examined from two viewpoints. One view is from above. Managers are accountable for meeting the obligations they have made to *their* managers. The other view is from below. Managers are accountable for meeting commitments arising from the nature of their relationships with their subordinates. That is, they are accountable for providing their employees the support and the working conditions they need to be able to deliver on *their* accountabilities.

All managers must be accountable for:

1. Securing their employees' commitment to pursue ambitious and attainable goals.
2. Providing the authorities and resources their subordinates need in order to deliver on their ambitious commitments (as discussed previously in relation to QQT/R).
3. Ensuring that employees do, in fact, meet all of their fixed and relative organizational obligations or that they get managerial agreement to change them.
4. Calling subordinates to account if they fail to meet their obligations.
5. Giving subordinates constructive feedback about their effectiveness and formally appraising their performance.
6. Coaching subordinates to enhance their effectiveness to help them work as closely as possible to their full potential and the role's maximum required effectiveness.

These six core accountabilities are obviously linked, and all of them serve the same broad function: to ensure that employees deliver fully on their obligations to their managers, and that, by extension, managers fully meet their obligations as managers to support the organization to achieve its overarching goals.

Okay, but how do these six accountabilities play out at work?

A manager is accountable for being clear with her subordinates, both by specifying QQT/R and other accountabilities and, as we shall see, by communicating to employees the larger context surrounding their accountabilities.

A manager is accountable for her subordinate's outputs. A manager cannot go to his boss and say, "Gee, I'm sorry, but I can't deliver on my commitments to you. Charlie, who works for me, said he was going to hit his targets, but he screwed up, and that's not my fault." When a manager tries to pawn his own failure off on a subordinate, his superior knows it and should be thinking (or saying), "The buck stops with you about your subordinates' results." You might say the manager's credo for the 21st century must be: *No excuses about your subordinates' QQT/Rs! No surprises about your own QQT/Rs!*

Similarly, a manager is accountable for his subordinates' proper use of delegated resources. If Jayne wrecks a piece of equipment or is injured because she wasn't properly trained, or if Louis sexually harasses Diane, their manager can't go to his boss and say, "It's the employee's fault or it's HR's problem." Managers are accountable for the on-the-job health and safety of their subordinates. It's not HR's job. It's not OSHA's job. Even if developing employee health and safety processes *is* HR's job, any specific employee's welfare isn't their direct accountability. The numbers of managers who have ignored employee complaints about poor conditions or dangerous equipment are legion, and everyone has regretted their neglect.

To accomplish this, a manager must be accountable for giving his subordinates the authority they need in order to deliver on *their* obligations. Holding employees accountable for achieving a goal that they haven't been given the authority to achieve is an exercise in magical thinking by the manager. Invariably, this generates stress, frustration, and resentment in employees. Even when the result is obtained, it is usually at the cost of suboptimizing the overall organizational results.

So, what's a manager to do? Every manager is accountable for ensuring that his or her subordinates are adding value to the organization at the level required by their roles and for the continual enhancement of subordinate effectiveness. Managers do this through feedback and coaching to help each subordinate systematically expand his level of skilled knowledge, focus, discipline, and commitment, and his working maturity. It is in creating excitement among subordinates about contributing their full measure of value and giving them the support and conditions to master their work successfully that managers fully and accountably leverage the potential of their people.

When Accountability ≠ Authority

Marie Flynn, an editor at an economic consulting firm, was accountable for getting an update on the U.S. economy out to clients by the tenth day of every month. She found this goal difficult, and at times impossible, to accomplish, because the economists who wrote the articles for the update rarely finished their pieces on time. Both Marie and the economists were subordinate to the chief economist, Mike Whitfield. When Marie told Mike that she couldn't get the update produced on time unless the economists got their articles to her on time, Mike said, "Crack the whip!" Marie asked incredulously, "What whip?" Mike casually replied, "Just tell them if they don't get their articles in on time, you can't get the update out on time."

Of course, the editor had told the economists that many times before. Yet Mike would not hold them individually accountable for getting their articles finished on schedule. And Marie, the editor, who had zero-defined authority over the economists, remained thwarted until the day she resigned.

The reverse of this problem—authority without accountability—also occurs. For example, an employee may be given authority over processes, people, or other resources but not be held accountable for how well he or she is deployed or what results are achieved. When that happens, eventually that employee becomes self-absorbed and develops a sense of entitlement. Employees are given authority so that they can accomplish an organizational goal, not so they can "have something to play with." As we shall see, accountability must always be defined, commensurate with the authority delegated.

Filling the Hole with Responsibility

Another common mistake is confusing accountability with responsibility. In the purest sense, responsibility is what an individual demands of himself or herself. It has to do with one's conscience, aspirations, and internal standards. Accountability has to do with specific obligations one has to another individual based on mutual commitments each has made to the other. Unfortunately, most organizations use these words interchangeably as a way to make people feel accountable when they don't actually have the authority necessary to be held accountable.[3]

When employees are unclear about their accountabilities or lack the authority they need to deliver on their accountabilities, they fall back on their own sense of personal responsibility. Because most companies have highly responsible employees, those employees take it upon themselves to get the job done, usually at considerable cost to themselves and their co-workers and always, as a consequence, end up suboptimizing overall organizational effectiveness.

Gino Ferrone, a client of ours in the metal fabricating business, had recently promoted Sam Travers, a 12-year veteran, to assistant superintendent, a significant position in production. Since that promotion, Sam had grown irritable, disruptive, and dysfunctional. His leadership style included yelling, threatening, cursing, and even kicking cans around. This behavior had begun only after Sam's promotion.

In the course of working with the company's senior executives on other organizational issues, I was asked to have a talk with Sam. To my surprise, I found him to be courteous, reasonable, intelligent, and mature. If anything, he was fully aware of his so-called accountabilities—and chief among them was keeping his area's machines operating at 80 percent of capacity, or more. However, the machine operators were subordinate to their shift supervisors, not to Sam.

Sam told me, "The operators are afraid that if a machine breaks down from being cranked too high, they'll catch hell from their supervisors. I'm not their real boss. They know that. Their real bosses are their supervisors, who can dock their pay, write them up, suspend them, and fire them. No matter how clearly I describe the reasons for, and importance of, speeding up the machines, they always turn a deaf ear."

I asked Sam about the supervisors' role in getting the machines to run at the higher rate. "They're always busy fighting fires," he said. "They either dismiss my concerns or tell me to handle it myself."

Sam thought for a moment and chuckled nervously. He said, "Before long, I started getting upset. When I did, when I yelled and screamed and put up a fuss, the operators did what I wanted, at least for a day or so. They'd keep those machines going faster. So that worked, the way I see it."

The way I saw it, Sam felt he had little choice. He had no managerial authority over the operators. Yet he felt responsible for getting those machines running at 80 percent or better.

I leveled with Gino and other senior managers. "Sam Travers operates the way he does because of the situation you've placed him in," I said. "He sounds off on the machine operators because he feels it's the only way he can get results. Believe it or not, from his perspective, he's acting *responsibly.*"

Initially they were astonished, but they soon grasped the distinction between accountability and responsibility—and especially the importance of delegating the authority proportionate to the accountability.

An employee who is working hard but not getting the intended results, or who is achieving results only at considerable cost to co-workers, subordinates, or the larger organization, is probably acting responsibly. With such individuals, you must first review their accountabilities and set them in the context of the company's goals. The next crucial step is to ascertain whether the person has both the commensurate authority and the resources to get the job done. Gaps in the accountability-authority equation may be resolved simply or may require rethinking the alignments in your structures and processes.

Genesis

Where do organizational accountability and authority come from in the first place? And what are their economic, intellectual, and moral roots?

Originally, people formed organizations in order to accomplish tasks that they could not accomplish alone. Management is the art and science of getting things done through others. Employment organizations are one type of work organization, namely managerial leadership systems. And because the authority gets distributed down such systems (manager to subordinate manager to subordinate, and so forth), and because accountability must always accompany delegated authority, managerial systems are inescapably accountability hierarchies. This is not true of partnerships (where the owners do the work themselves), universities (where tenured professors are not employees), or churches (where priests are ordained members of the organization).[4]

In a corporation, authority originates with the shareholders. By virtue of their investment in the enterprise, they own it. They assume the risk and do so with the expectation of financial gain. The shareholders elect a governing body— the board of directors—to represent their interests and to oversee the management of the company.

In the process, the shareholders delegate authority to the board of directors to appoint a CEO and, through their voting rights, hold the board accountable for the CEO's actions and results. If the shareholders don't approve of the board's strategic definition and resource delegation or of the results delivered to them by the CEO, they can vote the members of the board out. The board, in turn, authorizes the CEO to use the company's resources in ways that will maximize the value of the shareholders' investment, and they are held accountable by the shareholders for ensuring that the CEO does so. Obviously, the CEO cannot do this alone, so he delegates authority to his senior executives and holds them accountable for working effectively on their obligations in marketing, finance, operations, and the other functions of the company and for meeting their commitments—no surprises. Those executives, in turn, delegate to their subordinate managers and hold them accountable for delivering on their obligations.

This process of delegating accountability and authority extends all the way down the hierarchy, through the levels of management, to supervisors, and ultimately to employees who have no subordinates. The essence of the system is a linked chain of authority delegation, employee discretion, and accountability. Each A-B-C link (shareholder-director-CEO, CEO-EVP-VP, superintendent-supervisor-operator) cascades down the organization. Because any chain is only as strong as its weakest link, every manager and every employee at every level must be held accountable for delivering on both their fixed and relative obligations.

The Good, the Bad, and the Ugly

Hierarchy is intrinsically neither good nor bad. It is simply a feature of all employment organizations. That's why I'm amused at, and disheartened by, the fads over the last decade that tout flat organizations, self-managed teams, and small self-contained, amoeba-like work groups, claiming that they are by nature efficient and nimble. When there is no means for ensuring individual accountability in these flattened organizations, self-managed teams, and small work groups, getting results is like a crapshoot. And what good is being nimble if you cannot depend on the results?

Although hierarchy is a characteristic of all managerial leadership systems and is, by its nature, neither good nor bad, there are definitely good and bad hierarchies.

Bad hierarchy is what we usually call bureaucracy. It's red tape, slow movement, inflexibility, too many layers of management, and too many managers who don't add value. It's lack of accountability, or lack of clarity about accountability, or misplaced accountability. It's accountability without authority or authority without accountability. It's command and control—withholding decision-making authority, adding layers of approval, and rendering people virtual robots. Any one of these will result in bad hierarchy. When they occur in concert, it gets ugly.

Interestingly, bad hierarchy can be found in companies of all shapes and sizes. Flat organizations often stretch management talent and other resources too thin to exploit all available opportunities, or even to execute day-to-day operations effectively. And small companies are legendary for overblown bosses who can't or won't delegate the authority necessary for their people to get the job done themselves.

Good hierarchy exists in companies with properly distanced levels of management. It is found in organizations with properly defined roles populated by people whose capabilities match their roles. Good hierarchies feature managers who develop clear, mutually agreed-upon accountabilities with their subordinates. In good hierarchies, managers give their subordinates the authority to take and implement decisions needed to fulfill their obligations. Good hierarchy doesn't inhibit judgment, creativity, and decision-making. On the contrary, it encourages individual initiative by giving people a clear mission and the right resources, clear boundaries, and enough of what I call *mental elbow room* to add their unique value.

To see who's getting it right, take a look at the annual lists of companies in *Fortune* or *BusinessWeek*. Scan the *Fortune* lists that rank companies by EBITDA (earnings before interest, taxes, depreciation, and amortization). Until a few years ago, Ford Motor Company ranked in the lowest 20 percent. The company had 12 layers of management, and that was more than it needed. The company has since started to pare down with a target of no more than eight levels of management.

In the pharmaceutical industry, Johnson & Johnson has long been viewed as a highly effective and nimble organization. The company is also among the least centralized, and many people chalk up J&J's success to decentralization. That, however, is not exactly the reason. Rather, it is that the company is properly structured and properly managed to allow each business-unit head sufficient freedom to compete in his or her own marketplace, but always within the collective corporate strategy. Success doesn't depend on centralization or decentralization. It depends on being properly structured and properly managed.

Accountability Is a Two-Way Street

Both managers and their subordinates are accountable for delivering on their obligations. We have examined these mutual obligations and focused on the importance of delegating authority along with accountability. We've also seen the distinction between accountability and responsibility and looked into the nature of accountability hierarchies. The burning question now hovering in the back of your mind must certainly be, "Okay, what can I do about all this?"

That's where leadership comes in. As you know, lead is a verb. But it is also an acronym that stands for Leverage, Engage, Align, and Develop. As you will see in the next chapter, these are the four cornerstones of accountability leadership.

---

[1]To protect client confidentiality, I've used pseudonyms in examples drawn from the practice of The Levinson Institute (as opposed to those from the public domain). All of the cases involve actual people, companies, and business situations.

[2]The use of QQT/R throughout this book comes from Elliott Jaques's definition of a task in *Requisite Organization.*

[3]Elliott Jaques first established this clear distinction in *Requisite Organization.*

[4]Elliott Jaques first analyzed and reported these distinctions in *A General Theory of Bureaucracy.*

Chapter 2

LEAD People to Accountability

No general can win a war alone. No captain can sail a schooner single-handedly. No architect can build a skyscraper by himself. And no executive can operate an extensive organization as an individual contributor. Leadership of any kind—managerial, military, moral, religious, political, or educational—requires leveraging the intelligence, skills, behavior, and potential of many individuals in order to accomplish something greater than the leader or the individuals could achieve on their own. At its best, leadership leverages the full potential of the human resources that have been organized to accomplish a goal.

In setting direction, the leader, in effect, says, "I am trying to accomplish something that I cannot accomplish on my own. But with your input, commitment, judgment, and energy we can collectively accomplish this." The leader must ensure that all participants understand what he is trying to accomplish, why he is trying to accomplish it, and the roles they play in accomplishing it. In this way, the leader maximizes the leverage that is the essence of managerial leadership.

That last point warrants emphasis. Leverage is the essence of leadership. The primary role of the manager is to leverage resources—and here we are talking mainly about human resources—to achieve a goal. That is the added value that a manager contributes to an enterprise.

Gimme an L!

At the end of Chapter 1, I said that the acronym LEAD stands for Leverage, Engage, Align, and Develop. If leverage is the essence of leadership, then what are the levers? They are engagement, alignment, and development.

It begins with an understanding of leverage, which usually takes time and experience and requires reflection. In fact, even many seasoned managers do not understand their full role in their organizations. They were not hired to "make sure people are working" or to "tell people what to do" or to attend meetings or just to think great thoughts. They were hired to leverage the creative capabilities of their people—to make the total result of all their contributions greater than the sum of the parts.

A lever is a simple tool that enables someone to lift a heavy object higher than he could on his own. Archimedes said that with the proper leverage, he could move the universe. Similarly, leadership—when properly practiced—enables people in a company, department, or team to accomplish more than they could on their own.

In contrast, when a company is poorly led, or employees fall into disarray, exhibit poor morale, and shift into "exit mode," managers can only appeal to the employees' sense of personal responsibility—to do the best job they can on their own, as described in Chapter 1. But they will never achieve the level of results that they *could* if they were getting the lift that comes with leverage.

The concept of leverage places the burden of lifting the organization where it belongs: on leadership. The levers are in management's hands. The art and science and challenge of leadership is the practice of using the levers of engagement, alignment, and development to lead people to achieve something that would otherwise not be possible.

Gimme an E!

People are engaged in an enterprise when they have fully committed their hearts and minds to the work required by their jobs. Though straightforward, the notion of engagement often confuses many people. I believe the confusion stems from the popular image of a leader as someone who enthralls his audience by means of emotion. While leadership in an accountability framework does demand that the manager engage people's hearts and minds, it is a mistake to believe that effectively engaging people in their work depends primarily on the coercion or the charisma associated with emotional appeals.

Some managers and, I'm afraid, many business-book authors make this mistake, which amounts to confusing managerial leadership with political leadership. Political leaders must rely on coercion (which plays to people's fears) or charisma (which plays to their neediness). Political leaders often resort to this because they lack the positional authority that comes with a managerial role. They must craft their power from the will of the people. If, as a manager, political leaders are your leadership role models, you may well look to Attila the Hun and Machiavelli for helpful hints on coercion or try to project the charisma of Nelson Mandela or Margaret Thatcher. Or you may just chuck the whole idea of becoming a leader. After all, if you don't have the mind of an Abraham Lincoln, the voice of a Winston Churchill, and the authority of a Colin Powell, why bother?

Instead of coercion and charisma, effective managerial leaders actually have a much more reliable means of engaging people: the psychological contract between employer and employee. This psychological contract represents an implicit—often unspoken—understanding and agreement on what the company will provide, and what the employee will provide, to make the relationship work. It is not to be confused with an employment contract, which is a legal device that details what employers and employees owe each other. All managers and employees, including those with employment contracts, develop an assumed psychological contract with each other, whether or not they are consciously aware of doing so. In this chapter, I'll introduce this concept and its application, and in Chapter 4 you will fully examine how to use it to engage your people in their work.

Gimme an A!

People can be fully engaged in their work, but unless their thoughts, decisions, and actions are aligned, their work will do the organization little good. Employees are aligned when they understand the relationship between their activities and goals and those of their organization, managers, and co-workers—and then act on that understanding. Engaging people is a necessary start, but it is only a start.

Consider any team sport and what makes a team great. A star athlete is a wonderful asset. Yet a great team works as a team. Its coach discourages grandstanding, ball-hogging, and selfish play, because he understands that team wins, rather than personal records and achievements, are what really counts at the end of the day. So each player must be aligned with that team goal. Each player also must know his position and remain constantly aware of how his position relates to the other positions in various situations—and always act with his own objectives and the team's overall objectives, simultaneously, in mind.

Let's say a batter hits a high-bouncing grounder between first and second base. The players automatically execute a whole series of shifts. The first baseman lunges for the ball, misses it, and skids along on his belly. The right fielder, charges for it, as the center fielder moves to back him up in case it takes a bad bounce and he misses it. The second baseman runs over to cover first base while the first baseman gets up off the turf. The shortstop covers second base and readies himself for the throw from the outfielder, who hopes to hold the base runner to a single. Meanwhile, the pitcher backs up the shortstop in case the throw from the outfielder is high.

Your average Little Leaguer grasps this. Yet this level of teamworking functionality remains elusive to most managers and employees—for a very simple reason: lack of context. A game, any game, sets the context within which people must function and interact. The rules, boundaries, positions, and plays all contribute to clear context. Within such a clear context, people understand the goal, their role in achieving it, others' roles in achieving it, the relationships between those roles, permissible moves, and the leader's expectations governing all of this. That creates alignment. (You'll examine the basic principles of alignment in this chapter and elaborate them in Chapter 5.)

Gimme a D!

Managers must be held accountable for effectively developing their people, their human resources, just as they are accountable for developing all other resources. Nonetheless, employee development has long received short shrift in U.S. business. Although many companies profess deep belief in development and in training, performance appraisals, job enrichment, and career guidance, these take a distant second to the "real work" of running the day-to-day operation and hitting revenue, production, and profit targets. When it comes to employee development, the management mantra has long been, "That's HR's job" or "I'll do it if I have any time left at the end of the day." Now in our current environment of job-hopping, headhunting, multiple careers, independent contractors, and companies determined to keep as much of their workforce as possible off the books, employee development has deteriorated to a new low.

Yet the same companies bewail high turnover, recruitment costs, and a "talent gap"—all of which they have been instrumental in creating. Employers rightly cite diminished employee loyalty as a force behind these trends. However, employers bear an even greater responsibility for creating those trends by failing to demonstrate their commitment to effectively developing employees in their current work roles and for their future careers.

The HR function can provide useful tools to support, but it cannot be held accountable for individual employee development. However, the tools that HR traditionally provides—position analysis, training, performance standards, compensation analysis, employment policy, career guidance, succession-planning processes, and so on—can indeed be valuable when applied within a framework of managerial accountability for employee development.

Managers must be held accountable for developing their subordinates and for helping them to realize their potential. This demands an accurate knowledge of the employee's potential, and it requires thoughtful, mature coaching and mentoring of employees to reach that potential. I'll sketch in the outlines of a proven approach to employee development in this chapter, fill in the picture in Chapter 6, and delve more deeply into this important issue in Part III.

LEAD!

LEAD represents a total system, and a way of thinking and acting, that will enable you to be a far more effective manager and leader. It starts with the concept that managers exist to leverage people's potential so that they can achieve more than they could alone. To get this leverage, managers must engage their employees' enthusiastic commitment and ensure that they are in alignment with the organization and one another. To maintain leverage over the long term, managers must develop their people's capabilities to be able to apply their full potential to the work of the organization. All within an accountability framework!

Let's look more closely at each element of the system:

- Leveraging potential.
- Engaging commitment.
- Aligning judgment.
- Developing capacity.

To Achieve New Heights, Try Leverage

What could be worse than an employee who performs his job like an automaton? What value would a worker contribute if she never exercised real judgment when doing the work of her role? What is work, anyway?

Work, in physics and engineering, is the application of force to an object over the distance the object moves. Correspondingly, work in a managerial system is the application of mental forces to an assignment over the time it takes to complete that assignment. Work is the exercise of judgment and discretion to get something done.[1] (For years, IBM's motto was simply, "Think!")

The fixed accountabilities (from Chapter 1) are required job-specific outputs and working limits. They define the assignment and the rules of engagement surrounding the assignment. Employees are accountable for delivering fixed commitments precisely, unless their managers agree to modify these commitments. The fixed accountabilities are necessary to keep the organization focused and on track.

The relative accountabilities, on the other hand, are reflections of the value that employees are accountable for adding in their roles—value added by their application of judgment and discretion. This is the key to understanding how managers become effective leaders. Managers must fully leverage the collective mental force of their people in order to elevate the whole organization's power to deliver value to the customer and, ultimately, to the shareholder.

Thus when some managers say that they employ people to produce outputs, my response is, "In part, yes; in part, no." It is true that your employees must commit to, and deliver on, outputs. But what you are really paying for is their creative initiative to figure out how to deliver the greatest value possible in their role *while* meeting their output and process boundary commitments.

Other managers remark that they are paying for knowledge, experience, and skills. To this I also say, "In part, yes; in part, no." Pure judgment (as in problem-solving ability) without skilled knowledge is akin to a carpenter without tools: great blueprint, but no structure! When you hire a carpenter, you are not primarily hiring his tools. You are hiring his capabilities to do good carpentry; the tools are assumed. So it is with employing people to apply their judgment. You must make sure they have the skilled knowledge required for the role and, as we will discuss later, you are also accountable for helping to further develop their skilled knowledge. But they use their judgment to complete assignments and add value to the organization.

Still other companies say what they really hire is passion. They recruit people with a competitive instinct. I still say, "In part, yes; in part, no." Effective leaders seek out and increase the enthusiastic commitment of their people, but commitment to do what? It is the commitment to fully, effectively, and passionately apply their judgment to solve the problems necessary to help the organization deliver value.

So you see, leadership is all about leveraging the individual judgment of each subordinate and the collective judgment of all employees working together within an accountability framework.

One central feature of all the managerial systems that we will explore in this book is that work at different levels in the organization reflects innately different levels of complexity.[2] A key part of a manager's work and thinking consists of incorporating the complexities of her manager's work and thinking into hers. Next, she translates her own thinking down to a level of complexity that is useful to her subordinates. Each manager, at each level, is a fulcrum in the leveraging of the capability of her own unit for her manager. The system becomes, in effect, a useful—and lawful—pyramid scheme.

In a residential real-estate development company, for example, the CEO deals with more complexity than the architect, who deals with more complexity than the general contractor, who deals with more complexity than the carpenters, electricians, and plumbers. The CEO must give the architect his thought about the size and types of homes for their target market, price points and costs, characteristics of the home sites, and so on. The architect considers this in designing the houses and then translates that to a level of complexity that is useful to the general contractor when he looks at the plans. What happens if the backhoe operator digging the foundation hits a huge boulder? He, the crew, and perhaps the contractor would be expected to figure out how to remove it in a way that is consistent with the building plans and the look and feel of the development, without involving the architect or the CEO.

In fact, setting context[3] is the most important leadership practice a manager can deploy to leverage subordinate judgment. It consists of including your subordinate in your own thinking and in your manager's thinking, and then incorporating your subordinate's thinking into yours. It improves upon the quality of a manager's plan and it helps a subordinate to think, plan, and make adjustments intelligently—that is, in a way that best supports the bigger picture.

If the essence of leadership is leveraging potential, then what are the tools for leverage? The first is to engage the enthusiastic commitment of one's people to apply that potential.

Getting Started

As free-thinking, intentional creatures, human beings must willingly commit themselves to apply their judgment to get the results required by the job. If they are not committed, then their minds are elsewhere, focused on the coming weekend, the health of their portfolio, or the progress of their job search. When your subordinates are engaged, you maximize the judgment and esprit de corps they bring to the job. The greater the engagement, the greater their commitment to apply their judgment to the job, within an accountability framework.

We said earlier that instead of coercion or charisma, managers have a more reliable means for engaging people: negotiating healthy psychological contracts. This term, now in widespread use, was coined more than 40 years ago by Dr. Harry Levinson,[4] progenitor of The Levinson Institute, to describe the implicit elements of mutual need worked out between employers and employees. Dr. Levinson founded the Institute in 1968 to help organizations and the people in them adapt effectively to competitive and changing environments.

The psychological contract rests upon a foundation of mutual commitment to each other's success. In fact, the degree to which someone will commit himself to making someone else (in a relationship) successful is always in direct proportion to the evidence that the other party is committed to making him successful too. Commitment requires reciprocity and trust.

Although employees experience a psychological contract with the entire organization, their immediate managers forge the real relationships that embody the contract on behalf of the company. Negotiating strong, mutual, and reciprocal contracts requires that managers attend to what their employees value, how they define success, and what demonstrates to them that the organization supports their pursuit of success.

As a general guide, employees perceive their companies as being committed to their success when they provide:

1. A safe, healthy work environment.
2. Respectful, trustworthy relationships.
3. Regular opportunities for providing input to the organization, its goals, and one's own assignments.
4. Valuable, personally meaningful, and challenging work.
5. The resources and authorities necessary to meet accountabilities.
6. Assistance in reaching one's full potential within the organization.
7. Recognition and appreciation of one's contribution.
8. Fair compensation.
9. An organization's commitment to its own success and perpetuation.

If an employee—or your entire workforce—fails to demonstrate the level of engagement sought, use the preceding list as a diagnostic checklist. Invariably, at least one and usually more of these elements will be your clue to remedial action.

However, you must consider these conditions in relative terms and with the needs of the company, as well as the employee, in mind. A safe, healthy environment means one thing in a financial institution and another on an oil rig. An oil rig will never be as safe as a bank. Whatever it means in a particular business, employees should be kept as safe as possible and fully informed about risks and hazards. Market forces determine fair compensation, but there are many ways to cast a fair, internally equitable compensation package. Providing meaningful work does not obligate a company to eliminate all tedium and drudgery from the workplace. A certain amount of it comes with any job (even the CEO's). Few employees expect on-the-job nirvana, and most can comprehend the constraints that companies face. Yet they expect a committed employer to provide the best possible conditions within those constraints. Good managerial leaders are attuned to the unique interests of their subordinates and the kinds of work and working conditions that could harness and release their enthusiastic commitment.

If a company provides these conditions to support its end of a healthy psychological contract, employees are all but certain to contribute the full measure of their judgment, energy, knowledge, and skills to the company's success.

Finally, it's worth mentioning that context setting and QQT/Rs—the quality, quantity, and timeframe of a deliverable, and the resource constraints surrounding it—is part of the psychological contract. The very process of jointly defining intentions and ambitious and attainable QQT/Rs creates engagement. Managers who, for whatever reason, only vaguely communicate individual accountabilities to subordinates abandon them wondering what they should be and worrying what will happen if they guess wrong. Employees actually prefer clarity when it is a product of constructive two-way communication. They do not want to be ordered around, which is why QQT/Rs must be thoughtfully defined, debated, and mutually decided. However, they do want clarity regarding a manager's expectations of them and regarding the resources a manager will provide so that they can meet those expectations. That mutual understanding, the product of defining QQT/Rs, encourages engagement.

The Line on Alignment

Engagement harnesses employees' commitment. Alignment enables employees to work effectively together to maximum overall advantage. Alignment occurs when employees are properly oriented along many dimensions—toward the organization's goals, toward their manager's thinking and intentions, and toward other members of the team.

Alignment enables employees to optimally use their judgment to craft, with others, the day-to-day, often minute-to-minute, adjustments that will best support management's thinking in light of changing conditions. This means searching not for the convenient solution or the one everyone can live with (a process Peter Drucker famously labeled "satisficing"), but rather searching for the best solution in light of the manager's thinking and overarching intentions. Such efforts produce the greatest degree of leverage.

Subordinates can use their own judgment to extend and amplify their manager's goals only when they fully understand the manager's thinking and intentions. That thinking and those intentions comprise the context in which employees work. Thus a manager sets context—and creates alignment—by communicating his thinking and intentions.

Alignment ensures that employees are not only accountable for accomplishing their own, individual missions—the QQT/Rs—but that they deliver their accountabilities in such a way that ensures they fit into, and support, the whole. With that framework, they can be expected to chart and continually adjust a course to the optimal solution between them. So in creating context, a manager brightens the light on the areas where employees should focus and dims it on areas where they do not need to focus.

Most managers do a spotty job of setting context. Even those who take time to clarify the purpose of an effort often fail to explain how their subordinates' roles fit together to support that common goal. When I ask senior executives how they set context for their companies, they often point to the mission statement. There it hangs on the wall in the cafeteria—having no more effect on employee behavior than the Code of Hammurabi. True context-setting demands that managers regularly, in two-way discussion, accurately convey their thinking and intentions regarding their own (and their manager's) goals, ways, and means, and their subordinates' roles, rather than post a barely comprehensible paragraph about quality and customers on the wall.

But wait, there's more. To be optimally useful, context must be translated into a more fully articulated decision-making framework within which subordinates can make optimal tradeoffs between them. With such a framework, employees not only understand the context in terms of their manager's thinking and intentions, but they also understand the umbrella of alternative logic within which they must operate. This does not necessarily require developing detailed all-encompassing decision trees. Instead, it involves managers and their subordinate team members clarifying the "rules of engagement" to a sufficient degree that supports individual and collective creativity within an overarching plan.

In developing a decision-making framework, the manager and his team in effect say, "Having grasped the thinking and intention here, let's take time to identify the three, five, or 10 critical things to consider when we have to make a decision that involves outputs or resources in common." Then those considerations must be prioritized: Which is most important? Second most important? Third? Ideally, these should then each be assigned relative weights and upper and lower limits (which I'll discuss in Chapter 5).

The decision-making framework guides subordinates when they must make tradeoffs between them, involving key dimensions of the mission: revenue, costs, profits, quality, quantity, timeliness, customer satisfaction, or an objective such as winning a new market. The framework supports their making judgments in relation to each other and helps them to deal with a manageable level of complexity. Thus, to be useful, the framework must be constructed at a level of concreteness or abstraction appropriate to the type of judgment the subordinates are expected to exercise and the level of complexity they are qualified to address.

Simply going through the process of setting context and developing a decision-making framework does a lot to advance alignment in an organization. However, the result is as important as the process. The process creates alignment, but it is the quality of the context and decision-making framework that maintains it.

The Developing World

Almost all employees want to reach their full potential in their careers. If they see scant evidence of their company's serious commitment to their development, they conclude that they are on their own. Put another way, if the company violates its psychological contract by failing to develop its employees, why would they commit themselves to developing the company?

Employee development, as a continual, career-long process, represents the surest path to a workforce that functions with enthusiastic commitment at its full potential. If there truly is a talent gap (which I believe there is) and companies cannot find and retain enough high performers (which I believe they cannot), then senior executives need to start taking employee development seriously. This means understanding what development entails, creating a talent-pool-development system, and holding each manager accountable for effectively developing her own employees—both in role and in careers.

An employee cannot readily plan to develop to his full potential, nor can you help him to do so, unless you have a good idea of what that potential is. The purest handle you can get on an employee's potential involves assessing his ability to handle complexity, which might be termed his capacity for complexity.[5] This point is quite important, because position levels in organizations are closely related to the complexity of the tasks and the kind of judgment involved in the work of those positions. You will examine ways to gauge an employee's potential in Chapter 6 and explore the matter more deeply in Part III. For now, please accept the notion that potential can indeed be accurately assessed and that this holds important implications for the development process.

Broadly, the tasks of employee development fall into two areas: developing subordinates in their current positions (through coaching) and developing skip-level subordinates to improve their fit for higher-level positions in the future (through mentoring). In other words, managers must be accountable for coaching their immediate subordinates and for mentoring their subordinates' subordinates.

Rather than coaching, mentoring, and developing employees, many managers and HR professionals now blatantly tell employees, "You are responsible for developing yourselves. Here are the resources, the courses, the videos, the Web sites. You're on your own, so go to it!" That is not employee development; it is abdication. And as always, managerial abdication has a price. Failure to actively help employees develop to their full potential limits their growth, their earnings, and their functionality. It also condemns the company to expensive rounds of hiring, orientation, and high turnover. Compounding the problem for companies that have acquired poor reputations for development and promotion is their greater difficulty of recruiting solid, ambitious new employees in a tight labor market. At the end of the day, the lack of a systematic and accountable approach to employee development sharply limits a company's talent pool, and thus its organizational effectiveness.

These problems are all avoidable as long as managers understand and value the open secret of high-performing companies: bringing the same dedication to the work of developing their people as they do to engaging them and aligning them.

What It Takes to LEAD

The system that I have labeled LEAD lacks the iron-fist approach of the old command-and-control style of management, as well as its paternalism and its limited view of employee potential. LEAD also eschews the passive let-a-thousand-flowers-bloom approach associated with employee empowerment, self-directed work groups, and similar laissez faire reactions to command and control.

Instead, LEAD begins with a clear mandate for managers to leverage their people to their highest levels of achievement, as individuals and as a group. LEAD recognizes that managers will draw forth employees' best efforts not by the unilateral issuing of orders, but by enthusiastically engaging their employees' commitment in their work. The primary tools for achieving engagement are QQT/R and the psychological contract between manager and subordinate. Furthermore, LEAD aligns those efforts when managers construct with their subordinates a powerful context—conveying management's thinking and intentions—as well as practical decision-making frameworks. And finally, LEAD looks to the long-term value of the individual and the organization by holding managers accountable for effectively developing their employees to their fullest potential.

To implement LEAD, you need a clear view of your managerial role, the flexibility to adopt new viewpoints, and the patience and intelligence to learn new skills. You also need the energy and commitment to work with yourself

---

[1]Elliott Jaques, *Requisite Organization,* p. 13.

[2]The concepts of levels of complexity in organization, in work, and in thinking, used throughout this book, are taken from Jaques, *Requisite Organization.* They are also taken from Elliott Jaques and Kathryn Cason, *Human Capablity.*

[3]Setting context, as used throughout the book, is from Jaques, *Requisite Organization,* p. 99.

[4]Harry Levinson (with Charlton R. Price, Kenneth J. Munden, Harold J. Mandl, and Charles M. Solley), *Men, Management, and Mental Health,* p. 22.

[5]Jaques and Cason, *Human Capability.*

and your people, to try and fail and try again until the system becomes part of your everyday managerial-leadership practice. In addition, you need the leadership courage to establish LEAD as an accountability for every manager and to assess each manager's value—and right to remain a manager—against this standard. I have seen the efforts made to implement LEAD repay themselves many times over for hundreds of managers in scores of organizations.

In Part II, I'll delve more deeply into leverage, engagement, alignment, and development, examining the details of the system, and exploring practical applications of each element.

Part II:
Creating Accountability

In Part I, we examined the central role accountability plays in organizations and in managerial leadership. We also introduced a framework for leading accountably and creatively: the LEAD System.

In Part II, the focus will be on each of the four elements in the LEAD system: leverage, engagement, alignment, and development. In the process, you will learn how to promote accountability, capability, and productivity throughout a business organization by applying time-tested managerial leadership practices.

Chapter 3
Leveraging Potential

At Harry Cohn's crowded funeral, Red Skelton quipped that Harry had obviously been right when he said, "Give the people what they want, and they'll show up."

Cohn, the legendary cofounder of Columbia Pictures, held his screenwriters—and most everyone else—in contempt. If he walked past the writers' department and did not hear typewriters clacking away, or if he saw two writers pausing to chat about a problem in a script, he would yell at them to get back to work. During Cohn's dictatorial regime from the 1920s until his death in 1958, Columbia reportedly had the highest personnel turnover of any studio. Like all despotic bosses, Harry displayed little interest in having his subordinates exercise judgment. Though he achieved a high degree of success in his years at Columbia, it is clear he could have been far more successful had he done so.

Many managers today, unfortunately, share Harry Cohn's misunderstanding about work and what constitutes effective working—despite decades of purportedly enlightened management thinking. In today's world, getting all employees to add as much value as possible has become imperative. For managerial leadership systems to excel in today's competitive arena, success depends most often upon your ability to leverage the judgment of *everyone* on your team.

Most of us find it relatively easy to grasp the concept of physical work. Physicists define work as the application of force to an object over distance or Work = Force × Distance. Until now, there have been no comparable clear definitions or scientific metrics for intellectual work, which is essentially what employees are hired to perform. Because the outputs of intellectual work can range from plans, projects, or other specific time-bound deliverables, this kind of work could be viewed as the application of judgment to an assignment over the time required to complete it. This could translate into a related formula, namely: Work = Judgment × Time.

In this chapter we examine judgment and complexity, two work-related concepts that are central to effective managerial practices.

Got What It Takes?

To be effective in a job, a person must possess the type of judgment required to execute that job. Put another way, he or she must possess the mental capacity to handle the complexities of a particular role. Think of a role as a basket of assignments. Every employee has been delegated a wide array of QQT/Rs. Some are short-term and simple. Others may be mid-range in time but extremely complex. Others may be long-term and of intermediate complexity. The exercise of sound judgment and discretion is necessary in order to accomplish each of them. In addition, juggling all of them together—with opposing time and resource constraints—requires significant judgment.

This basic problem-solving ability is innate and often referred to as native intelligence. It is critical that every employee possesses, at a minimum, the level of mental capacity consistent with the size of his or her role.

Jack, a bright young engineer in one of our client companies, had mastered his manufacturing engineering position and was promoted to manufacturing superintendent, a lateral function. He had little previous management experience and training and he had even less exposure to logistics, production planning, materials handling, and other staples of manufacturing. Yet, with several months of on-the-job training and coaching, he had not only significantly improved his area's productivity, delivery-performance, and quality, but he actually raised the bar for teamworking and employee effectiveness.

How could Jack accomplish this without the pre-existing skilled knowledge? Al, Jack's predecessor, was also conscientious and hardworking. Was it Jack's strong work ethic alone? Or was it something else?

The answer can be found in Jack's mental capacity or "horsepower." Jack was "way smarter" than his previous role required. He was also smarter than his new role required him to be. It was this excess mental capacity that he brought to bear on understanding the basic principles of manufacturing and people management. Formal training in these areas just did not matter that much. The greater the computational power, the broader the bandwidth, the quicker and better the problems of any role can be solved. Recognizing Jack's capability reserve, the company then slated Jack to move up another rung. After 20 months in the superintendent job, Jack took over the director of engineering position for the plant. Senior management commended Jack for handling that transition smoothly.

Jack's experiences demonstrate that innate, individual capacity exists independently of any particular role or function and is transferable between them.

There have been major advances in our understanding of human capability and its relationship to the workplace over the past 40 years and, in particular, over the past 12 years. Most of this knowledge has been developed, tested, and applied by a brilliant social scientist, Elliott Jaques. He helped to differentiate among the core elements of human capability, which together determine whether someone is likely to be effective in any particular role. In particular, he was able to directly measure an individual's type of mental process, which determines his or her current potential.

As you will see later, this research supports an accurate and easy-to-administer approach to the assessment of employee potential and mapping of an organization's pipelines of future potential.

Complexity, Simplified

The job-grading racket is a multi-billion dollar industry, with wizards applying complex formulas and weighting mechanisms when determining pay, title, and so forth—all in the service of describing the kind of employee needed to do a kind of work. Why shouldn't we be able to approach that task in a far less complex manner? The first clue is to go back to our metaphor of a role as a basket of QQT/Rs. Is there something about any role's QQT/Rs that can inform us about its size or complexity?

As we've already seen, an assignment is called a QQT/R (for quantity, quality, time, and resources)—essentially the delegation of an output. It is a requirement to get something done at a defined quality standard and using specified resources, all within a targeted completion time. Developed by Jaques, it is a simple, yet powerful, mechanism for managers to accurately define assignments with subordinates.

As an individual plows through an assignment, it is the exercise of judgment that adds value. Work, after all, is all about unraveling the complexities inherent in any assignment. Work requires weighing how we might best get it completed, evaluating all the pros and cons of each path, deciding on the best plan based on many choices, and finally setting in motion its implementation.

One of the most significant contributions that Jaques made was identifying that, as one moves up in an organization, the work itself requires ever-higher levels of complexity. One measure of this complexity is how far out in time an individual in a position is accountable for delivering results. Long-term QQT/Rs, therefore, determine how far out that person must be thinking and implementing plans.

A machine operator, for instance, should be actively concerned with maintaining enough raw materials for his shift or, perhaps, over several shifts. The section's first-line manager, on the other hand, must think about the materials required for the orders on the books for the next several months. The area superintendent must plan for her accountabilities even further out, considering the improvements required in materials handling to meet all of the projected orders over the next 18 months. And so on, right up the line to the plant manager, who must think in terms of renegotiating the terms of his five-year contracts with the company's suppliers.

The biggest jobs require the most complex judgments: The higher the role in an organization, the more "weight of responsibility" will be experienced by those working in it. This reflects the degree of complexity of work in each role, complexity that increases quantitatively with each bigger role. In addition, Jaques discovered that, at certain points in the hierarchy, qualitative changes occur in the types of complexity that a role must deal with. At certain nodal points in the hierarchy roles become not only more complex, but change to a different and higher order of complexity. There are naturally occurring distinct levels of role complexity in every managerial hierarchy.

One practical application of these findings about organizational structures is that there appears to be an optimal distance between manager and subordinate roles, a distance close enough that ensures a manager can add genuine value and far enough that the subordinate has the "mental elbow room" to add real value as well.

Not Up to the Job?

Companies that ignore these natural principles of people-organizational alignment do so at their own peril. How many companies have collected seemingly inexhaustible lists of competencies and conducted massive 360-degree surveys of their employees in order to improve employee effectiveness? Nowhere in these processes is there any accurate appraisal of an individual's horsepower in relationship to the size of role he or she occupies. There is simply no language, no conceptual map, or no practical means for them to do so.

Here is a typical scenario. A fairly senior manager, who was quite competent and effective in his previous roles, was given a battlefield promotion. Because of the need for a "warm body" to follow through with a plan already in progress, not enough attention was paid as to whether this individual was big enough for the role. After the crisis passed, the CEO began to see numerous signs that the manager's division was continually getting into trouble. Overall, leadership from this individual seemed weak and the manager could never explain why he was having so much trouble.

After implementing our LEAD assessment process, the CEO came to the conclusion that this manager simply did not possess the raw mental capacity for the job he had been given. Only the process of evaluating the manager in this way provided upper management at the company sufficient insight to recognize what the core problem really was.

The CEO explained to me, "It was a fairly senior job and I wasn't getting the level of thought or leadership, in trying to push the envelope by that individual. So I finally came to the conclusion that he just didn't have the basic capability— the mental 'horsepower'—to succeed at the job."

Similarly, Martha, the president of a large advertising agency, asked Ed, her newly appointed HR vice president, to put together a white paper on personnel development. "This meant pulling together all of the high-potential people in our company and setting up a new process to develop career-planning strategies for them," she told me. Martha and Ed were then to meet three weeks later and discuss Ed's recommendations.

At the meeting, however, Ed offered a totally inadequate plan, one obviously not suitable for advancing *any* employee's career. Martha asked Ed to do it again, this time being more precise about the QQT/R. "Keep working at it," Martha said. "We'll meet again in another month." When the next meeting came around, Ed clearly had committed great effort into his plan, but still hadn't put an adequate—much less exciting—process together.

"At this point I had even more detailed discussions with Ed about what I wanted to do," Martha explained later, clearly exasperated. "We batted ideas around. But it was like there was no sense of creativity or innovation within this person, nor the ability to execute complex plans. Whatever I asked him to deliver to me within specific time periods never materialized. What fooled me was that he was quite knowledgeable and experienced. Yet, everything was inadequately done, not thought through, incomplete. Significant elements were missing. I concluded that he just didn't understand the importance of the missing elements or how to fit them all together to make the ultimate objective come through. He just wasn't big enough for the job."

Performance problems, strategic disconnections, and even dysfunctional behaviors often present as failures by employees to do what they "ought to be able" to do. In many cases, however, the real problem is that the employee was over-promoted by management. That cannot be his fault; rather, it is a failure of the organization and the selecting manager to accurately determine that the role was bigger than the candidate is. To add insult to injury, the employee is often fired for incompetence or blamed for failure to follow orders, when he had been extremely competent in previous roles that were equivalent in complexity to his capability.

Ed, by the way, was subsequently transferred to another role at a lower level of complexity and has performed quite well. Ed actually thanked Martha later for acknowledging her error in "prematurely promoting" him and also for helping him to get back on track with his career.

I Link, Therefore I Am

What is it that distinguishes the different types of judgments required at different organizational levels from each other? How are people different from each other in their native intelligence? Jaques's discovery in the early 1950s of these naturally occurring, distinct levels of work complexity launched him on a 40-year search for ways in which individuals' patterns of thinking are distinctly different.[1]

Most people, it turns out, have a remarkably keen sense when picking up evidence in others as to how "sharp" they are. Think about your own experiences getting to know a new group of people, say at a conference or a party. It usually doesn't take long (minutes? seconds?) to size people up, not only in terms of what they know, where they come from, what they like, and so on, but also in terms of cleverness, quickness, intuitiveness, and so forth. This is what I call a person's *force of logic.*

This force is the basis of human work. The force behind this logic is literally the ability to make and apply connections when trying to figure something out. Those possessing the mental force or horsepower to work at a level higher than others do so by making more complex connections between things and applying those connections when working on and solving problems. How can we gain access to and calibrate our impressions of how bright or capable someone is in making these connections? Once you understand these levels, why not assess people using them as your yardstick?

After his initial discovery of these levels, Jaques began asking managers, "At what level do you believe a particular employee currently has the potential to operate?" He found a remarkably high correlation between what various managers (at the same or at different levels from each other) said about the same individuals. He even found a remarkably strong correlation with what people said about themselves. Here are descriptions of the four mental processes that Jaques discovered:

- People considered to be able to handle only the lowest level of work in a company consistently construct their arguments by shot-gunning volleys of unconnected assertions at a problem. "I believe this is wrong because of this OR that OR this other thing OR maybe that thing over there!" they spout.

- Individuals considered to possess the potential to be effective at the next higher level employ a different type of logic. They can be observed tying different information points together and weaving them skillfully into a pattern or hypothesis—one that can then be tested and from which a novel solution can be constructed. "When you look at this AND that AND this other thing too, they all point to THIS conclusion," come their arguments. The difference between OR-OR reasoning and AND-AND reasoning is not unlike the difference between a policeman, who merely collects evidence, and a detective, who tests possible links between the clues and detects patterns that ultimately solve the crime.

- The third level of people, higher up still, requires an *if-then* connecting ability. Here the need for decision-tree types of logic or algorithmic thinking is clear. These people say, "Well, *if* this is true, *then* this must also be true. And *if* that were to be the case, *then* this next conclusion would apply."
- Individuals at the next higher level, the fourth, require a multiple, parallel array of logical pathways, a sort of mental orchestration of parallel decision-trees: "*If* this one line of reasoning makes sense, under one set of circumstances, and *if* a second and third make sense under different sets of circumstances, *then* putting it all together suggests an inter-relationship between them of the following nature...."

In the 1980s, Jaques went on to prove *repeating* patterns of the four mental processes at progressively higher levels of information complexity. Most adults use symbolic language. Fewer adults are capable of abstract-conceptual abilities. And very few adult geniuses have the ability to create new bodies of knowledge. Individuals who possess one of the four levels of adult symbolic language or one of the repeating four levels of adult abstract-conceptual abilities inhabit the world of work.[2]

In a related escalating pattern, the types of judgments required at each higher level involve one more complex link than the level below. In a weak moment, one could even paraphrase Descartes by saying, "I link, therefore I am!" Following are descriptions of the different orders of information complexity found in organizations:

- At the lowest two levels in most organizations, roles are accountable for implementing clearly defined processes with an aim toward adjusting and optimizing them.
- When we move up one or two levels, these roles are accountable for defining the requirements for those processes, as well as for developing and "resourcing" them, managing their individual flows, and orchestrating their integration.
- Going up two more levels, we encounter corporate strategic roles that function as creators and managers of assets. These strategic roles also are accountable for developing conceptual models for enhancing asset worth.
- Two more levels higher can be found only in large-cap global companies and super-corporations (essentially a group of multiple companies, with each company competing in multiple industries). You find these roles accountable for creating asset-enhancing systems, gearing them in relationship to long-term economic, social-political, and technological consumer requirements. These organizations are rapidly becoming the core wealth-creation vehicles of modern society.

Let the Manager Beware

Remember that the requisite level of innate problem-solving ability by itself is necessary, but not sufficient, to ensure effectiveness in any particular role. To complement this raw ability, one must also have sufficient experience, skilled knowledge, commitment, and maturity.[3] But without enough mental capacity, an individual will always be Peter Principled and have to whittle the role down to a size he or she can handle.

Companies need to be concerned, not only with over-promoting people, but also with the longer-term consequences of under-promoting them. Managers must ask themselves, "Am I keeping people in roles that are too small for them?" Operate this way over time and count on everyone suffering the consequences. In addition to feeling under-appreciated and under-utilized, for example, people chronically bored and frustrated will simply not sustain their morale, commitment, and confidence. Although in the short run organizations might realize net gains by filling their positions with persons possessing excess capacity, in the long run it is going to work against them, especially in the current environment, where it is so difficult to retain good employees. (The only exception might be when the higher-capacity person is moved into a lower rung deliberately as a developmental move and thus part of his longer-term career development strategy.)

An even more fundamental problem for organizations today is that they have such a hazy notion (if that) of defining roles objectively. Without the insights and scientifically driven discoveries about work and levels of complexity (described previously), it is no wonder that most organizations have as much trouble as they do. Instead, the typical company tends to organize around the people it has— periodically shifting its logics for structure as people fall in and out of favor— delegating only whatever work its current, and seemingly haphazardly selected, workforce can handle. This *non*-system of role-establishment and role-filling usually results in a decidedly unscientific crapshoot! Rather than organizing proactively, with sound engineering principles, to be in alignment with company strategy, such organization is carried out in a purely ad hoc manner.

Don't Just Think Outside the Box

Now we have enough information to begin tying together into a single framework, an approach to leveraging the potential of employee judgment to achieve optimal organizational objectives...accountably. The force employees are hired to apply is their judgment. But the nature of a managerial leadership system is that it is an accountability hierarchy. Thus, all companies must reconcile two properties: creativity (judgment) and control (accountability).

If we examine the trends in the field of management alchemy, the gurus and business schools have swung the pendulum repeatedly (every five to 10

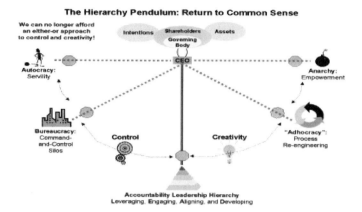

The Hierarchy Pendulum: Return to Common Sense

Accountability Leadership Hierarchy
Leveraging, Engaging, Aligning, and Developing

years) back and forth between creativity and control. The following Hierarchy Pendulum illustrates this. Now, it is creativity (self-directed teams, decentralization, empowerment, inverted pyramids, etc.). Then, it's control (TQM, centralization, control systems, etc.). There appears to be an assumption that these two properties are mutually exclusive, so management has to choose one over the other. Even Solomon could not be so wise.

Yet, they need not be incompatible at all. If we think clearly about the nature of managerial leadership systems, we can see that they are not only accountability hierarchies, but they are also judgment hierarchies. By this I mean that each manager at each level is accountable for meeting fixed commitments made to her manager (QQT/Rs and working within limits[4]), but how she meets them is up to her own judgment and discretion. If she decides on a plan that calls upon her to personally do one-third of the work and to delegate two-thirds of it, that's fine. She is still accountable for the whole QQT/R and making sure that the way she and her subordinates carry it out is within limits. In turn, she has the same set of expectations with her subordinates: deliver on your QQT/R, as agreed upon, no surprises, and within limits.

In this distributed, delegated, decision-making, accountability hierarchy, we have a systematic means for getting the optimal balance between creativity (each employee is encouraged to think creatively and take initiatives outside the box) and control (each employee must deliver on commitments precisely inside the box). When you throw into the equation the relative accountability for effective teamwork and cross-functional working, we can finally return to common sense: thinking creatively outside the box and acting accountably inside the box.

Linked Chains of Accountability and Judgment

When I ask managers what percentage of their time is spent doing what they were hired to do versus what percentage is spent chasing after problems created in other parts of the organization—problems that prevent them from doing their "real" work—I often hear figures as low as 20 or 30 percent, and I rarely hear figures greater than 50 percent. That means that well more than half of their time is spent compensating for holes in the linked chains of accountability and judgment in their organizations. No wonder so many managers say their companies leverage so little of their potential.

One of the most frequent structural causes of these weak links or disconnections turns out to be too many or too few managerial layers.[5] Think about the number of times you have worked for an organization that had too many levels. Most people knew it, right? "It takes forever to get a decision when we have to send the request up and down the flagpole." "That function has so many levels that its managers scurry around making work up to justify their existence." "My boss has so much time on his hands, he just hovers around and micromanages me." A central problem with too many levels is that managers are squeezed in too close to their subordinates to be able to add any real value.

Conversely, think about what happens when an organization (or a unit within) has too few levels. This may occur when it has grown so fast, that it literally outstripped its managerial skeleton. It often occurs when executives have given consultants free rein to blindly use a blunt ax to de-layer their company, allegedly to make it more efficient, but in reality to take out cost. Here the complaints may be different: "We don't have enough time or resources to get even the most basic work done." "My boss is so far removed and busy, I am left dangling in the breeze having to figure everything out for myself, with no direction or feedback." "We're always putting out fires." A central problem with too few levels is that managers are too busy and remote from their subordinates to be able to add any real value.

Wait a minute! Too close to add value, too far to add value? Does this imply that there is an optimal distance between a manager and his subordinates' roles that will increase the likelihood that the manager will add value and more fully leverage the potential of his people? Absolutely!

Let me try another metaphor: Imagine two 30-foot ladders being left outside overnight. Some pranksters come by with a saw, hammer, and nails. They saw off every other rung on one ladder and insert one between every rung in the other. Now, will it be more difficult to climb one or both ladders the next day? Sure! The "missing rungs" ladder is going to require a much greater stretch as you climb up or down; you'll have to be taller and have stronger muscles to move up and down with ease (read: brighter and more skilled knowledge and commitment). The "extra rungs" ladder is also going to be harder to climb, because you're going to want to skip rungs and put your foot where it would be natural to find the next rung. But because you can't know exactly how many rungs to skip, you're more likely to trip all over your own feet (read: non-value-adding positions in the hierarchy that you bypass only at your own peril).

So it is with managerial hierarchies. All employees benefit from having managers who are able to think at one level of complexity greater than they do. Thus, when our manager sets context for us, she's able to give us a more complex and valuable understanding of the overarching goals and the environment than we would be able to construct for ourselves. She's able to help us to think, plan, and execute smarter and in better concert with each other, and therefore able to fully leverage our potential—individually and collectively.

If our manager's position is in the same level of complexity as ours and is filled by someone who operates at the same level, he is not likely to add this kind of value. It will feel more like when a little kid experiences his big brother's advice more often than his parents'—he might as well be flying blind! Conversely, if our manager is operating at a level too remote from us, he may not be as effective in translating his world into terms that will be meaningful and useful to us. And we end up flying blind for a different reason.

Now you have it! Leveraging potential in a managerial system has very precise meanings. It has to do with the very nature of complexity and judgment. It has to do with the nature of accountability with its fixed and relative components. And it has to do with elements of organizational structure and role-establishment principles. But none of it is rocket science, and all of it is within your organization's grasp. Just think about it: If Harry Cohn had successfully leveraged Columbia's full potential in this way, perhaps his managerial acumen would be as revered today as Columbia's 1946 film *It's a Wonderful Life*.

The next three chapters will deal with three types of actions, things that managers must do, in order to capture this potential:

1. Engage the full and enthusiastic commitment of their people to apply their people's judgment.
2. Align their people's thinking, decisions, and actions with the larger picture and each other.
3. Develop their people's capabilities so as to most effectively realize and deploy their full potential.

---

[1] Elliott Jaques, *Requisite Organization,* p. 41.

[2] This research, also referred to later in this book, is reported in detail in Elliott Jaques and Kathryn Cason, *Human Capability.*

[3] Adapted from Jaques and Cason, *Human Capability.*

[4] The prescribed limits that Jaques described in *Requisite Organization.*

[5] Jaques, *Requisite Organization,* p. 40.

Chapter 4
Engaging Commitment

Francis Petro, a CEO who exemplifies accountability leadership, was brought in to turn around an international manufacturer of specialty metals. About six months into an organizational project with The Levinson Institute, he asked me to go out on the shop floor to see how things were progressing. I spoke with a number of workers to ask how they viewed the recent changes. Here is what I heard from two machine operators.

The first operator was clearly bitter: "I'm gonna leave as soon as I can find another job. It used to be fun coming to work. We'd catch up on the scores from the weekend games for a while, talk about some of the great plays, and plan for our fishing trips. Then we'd do some production, until break. After coffee and some smokes, we'd do a little more work, maybe break early for lunch. Now, with the new management, we've got to be at work at the machine when the bell rings, push hard all morning, maybe even miss the break and have a shortened lunch if we encounter problems. Even with my seniority and great benefits, I'm leaving."

The second operator was more typical: "Boy, this place was going downhill. Most of the employees came to work to catch up on their sleep. I was afraid the plant would be shut down and the whole town would be in trouble. Then Petro came in and shaped things up in a hurry. The supervisors got the message quickly after two were suspended and another one got fired for letting down on safety. Now, the super meets with the whole team every Tuesday morning for 30 minutes at change of shift. He fills us in on the improvement projects and the new safety campaign, lets us know how our delivery performance targets are coming, and lists the new sales and the customer feedback. He asks for our ideas and listens carefully. He seems to really think we have something to contribute. He's really on top of the problems and suggestions we raise; you can see how much better the equipment is running. Every time he walks by my station, he asks how I'm doing, asks if he can help with anything, and asks for my own ideas about how to make things work better. Last week, he asked if I'd be interested in taking some courses at the community college—at the company's expense—'cause he thinks I have the potential to move up. You know, it's really exciting what's happening around here!"

Did you notice the profound difference in the two responses? Despite what many people think, leadership is not a popularity contest. It is about leveraging the full potential of people and other resources in order to deliver maximum value to shareholders and customers. True leaders don't worry about whether people like them. It's much more important that their people respect the fact that they're engaged in serious work together. As Francis Petro says, "We're engaged in economic warfare with the competition. My job is to make sure my troops are fit for battle, to keep them safe and in top fighting order. Those that only want to play can do so elsewhere; my troops respect me and love to win! I expect a lot, but I give a lot. I have a dog at home that loves me; I don't need my people to love me. When they deliver to standard, I let them know. When they surprise me, I give 'em hell. They know it ain't personal." And, in fact, after one year, all of his employees would go into real battle for him, because Mr. Petro fights to ensure that *they* succeed. The battle cry was to increase safety, quality, and performance and, at the same time, to lower costs.

Consider the kind of leverage your company could achieve if its leaders fully engaged their employees' commitment. I'm sure you'll agree that all senior managers fervently desire committed employees. We read articles about companies where people spend extraordinary numbers of hours in their attempt to develop a product in record time so as to beat out their competition. We hear stories about employees so consumed with enhancing the performance of their companies that they appear to be thinking about how to improve company operations 24 hours a day, seven days a week. A few companies are legendary for their consistently superior levels of product quality and customer service that only a truly and extraordinarily committed staff can deliver. Legendary successes from companies such as L. L. Bean, Procter & Gamble, Southwest Airlines, and Toyota immediately come to mind.

Yet in many companies, one hears loud complaints from middle and senior managers about the lack of commitment, the low morale, and the strong cynicism among their employees. More and more companies are bemoaning their "brain drain": the difficulty in attracting, engaging, and retaining top quality talent. During the late 1990s, much of this problem was assigned to dotcom fever and the lure of fast money. Surely, the scarcity of labor that the Silicon Valley explosion created has contributed to people having more options and becoming more aware of—and dissatisfied with—the working conditions they find in their current positions. But is the issue really "greener grass" or a more fundamental lack of understanding of the basis for gaining employee commitment in the first place?

Most business school programs on management tell their students that the principal task of a leader is to "motivate her people." Scan *Amazon.com*'s search engine for books on leadership and you'll find the five or seven or 20 surefire secrets for motivating your workforce. Read the promotional promises from consulting companies specializing in compensation and they will tell you how to use rewards to motivate your people, with complex formulas tied to strategic deliverables. Inherent in all of these assertions is the assumption that workers need to be motivated—that they are basically inert or motionless automatons waiting to be bribed or cajoled into action. And we all know what animal that is most commonly thought of as requiring carrots and sticks to get it moving. Do we really think of our employees as jackasses?!

In 1973, Dr. Harry Levinson wrote *The Great Jackass Fallacy* to call attention to these superficial and mistaken notions about human motivation. People are not lifeless robots or computers. We are complex, multidimensional, intentional creatures. We are intrinsically motivated—by universal basic human needs as well as by highly specific individual wants, drives, and aspirations. The plain truth is that it is demeaning to say that managers must motivate their people.[1]

Managers must, instead, create the working conditions and sense of transcendent purpose that will harness and focus the natural enthusiastic commitment that all people bring with them. They must forge psychological contracts with their people backed up by a genuine commitment to help them succeed in ways that matter to them.

In this chapter, we will explore various myths and misperceptions commonly held about what employees really want from their organization and why they are self-limiting, at best, and self-defeating, at worst. We will then spell out the fundamental principles and applications that will allow managers to negotiate, and continually renegotiate, healthy and meaningful psychological contracts with their people—contracts that will ensure their full and enthusiastic commitment to support the organization in succeeding in its goals.

Harness *What* Motivation?

When you think back over all your days getting up in the morning before going to work, do any stand out as brighter and more energizing than others? Have there been times when you not only got up without the usual dread but actually felt eager to rush to work and resume something exciting and challenging from the day before? When you look back at your years of working and reflect on some of the more memorable days, can you recall moments of deep satisfaction and accomplishment that made a major effort worthwhile? These questions, as you can readily see, are designed to help you zero in on the heart of human motivation.

Motivation derives literally from "moving to action." What are the specific forces within the human mind that move people to action? Though there are many schools of thought that have something to say about this question, I have found a simple set of concepts most instructive. For example, human motivation comes from within. Each of us has a fairly well-developed personal and internal sense of what kind of existence is ideal. It's just that we are rarely consciously aware of it. Where does it come from? Psychology has taught us that as young children, we readily identify some of the core traits, qualities, and aspirations of those adults who surround us and on whom we depend. We internalize these attributes (usually after idealizing these adults) and they begin to form our own web of goals and aspirations that we consider to be "good."

As we grow older, we begin to make choices and, without realizing it, compare the alternatives and their meanings against this growing sense of "our ideal self." When we move in one direction and are successful, we feel good. If we're unsuccessful, we typically feel we have failed ourselves. This desire to live up to our own sense of what it means to be good or successful or true to oneself is the most important motivator of all human needs. But it is not the only one.

We also have powerful needs to master, to be challenged, to stretch ourselves, and to compete in addition to our needs to be liked, recognized, admired, and even cherished. These basic human drives are largely innate, constituting the basic temperament we see in very young children, but they are also significantly shaped by the people around us and by society in general. We learn very early on how our own culture views these drives and offers strong incentives to modify their expression in ways that others will accept. Acceptance by adults is especially important to children and acceptance by their peers is especially important to adolescents.

We also learn quite early whether we experience people as reliable, secure, and trustworthy, especially when we are heavily dependent on them to meet our needs. Our capacity to trust, on the one hand, and our tendency to feel guilty, on the other, are strongly shaped during the first several years of life. All of this learning, and the way it "moves us to action," comes together in shaping our view of the world. It also comes together in the way people view us. Our personality, in the end, is the composite picture of all of these attitudes and behaviors. It is who we are.

The need for managers to understand who their people really are is vital for one simple reason: We can't accurately know where someone is going unless we first know where he is coming from. Forging strong, mutually successful psychological contracts with one's subordinates requires an understanding of how each one of them views "becoming successful." This is because the psychological contract reflects a basic truth about human relationships: The degree to which one person will commit himself to support another in becoming successful depends largely on how much the other person demonstrates her commitment to making him successful.

Forging Psychological Contracts

What, then, are the basic outlines of the psychological contract? How should we examine the nature of the relationship between a manager and her subordinates and, at a higher level, between a company and its people? Harry Levinson, who coined the term "psychological contract"[2] in the 1950s, identified three dimensions of the company-employee and manager-subordinate relationship:

1. There must be a strong enough bond, built upon common purpose and values, to want to work together.
2. There must be a constructive, yet respectful, distance between the two.
3. There must be a mutual commitment to support the legitimate needs of one another during times of change.

A Bond Built on Common Purpose

The first prerequisite is common purpose. This is what most companies are trying to define when they craft a statement of purpose and mission. It is an attempt to describe "goodness," a set of values and aspirations that will provide a large enough umbrella for people to want to huddle under…together. How well does your company's mission statement speak to you? Is it specific enough to have personal meaning or so broad and filled with generalities that it might as well be motherhood and apple pie? As employees, we want to know what our company stands for and won't stand for, because we want to know whether it feels right to each of us. If you cannot relate to it at all or, worse, if you strongly disagree or disapprove of what your company stands for, no amount of forcing the engagement is going to correct the misfit.

A Constructive, Yet Respectful, Distance

Second, there is the mutual need for a healthy distance (control, recognition, and privacy) between the company and its employees. The employer has every right to decide on strategy, plans, and the specific QQT/Rs to meet those plans in order to meet shareholder expectations. Yet the employee, who has been hired to exercise judgment and add value while delivering on those QQT/Rs, properly wants to understand the bigger picture, to give input into shaping it, and to have an active role in helping his manager define those QQT/Rs, which the employee, after all, must commit to. And once agreeing and committing to the QQT/R, the employee needs the appropriate resources, processes, and working conditions with which to meet his accountabilities. The employee says, in effect, "If you (my manager) are going to decide on my accountabilities and are going to hold me accountable, then you must give me the necessary authority (that is, control) to meet them."

Similarly, every employer has the right to expect that its employees will attempt to represent its goals, means, and values well to others—both inside and outside the company. Differences of opinions will be dealt with maturely, candidly, and openly and employees will show mature respect for the diverse range of points of views of others. They will not speak ill of the company or people within the company and they will not undermine others by going behind their backs. Employees have the right to know where they stand with the company, to have their contributions properly acknowledged, and to have their legitimate needs for recognition, support, and development respected. It takes months and years to build trust and mutual respect, but it takes only minutes to destroy it.

There must also be a reciprocal understanding of, and respect for, the other's legitimate needs for privacy. Employers have trade secrets, confidential strategies, and even skeletons in the closet that they have a right to expect their employees will respect. Employees need to have a life of their own outside the company and a right to a certain measure of privacy inside the company. The recent wave of e-mail and Web site–tracking initiatives undertaken in many companies has created a significant backlash of mistrust and resentment among employees who feel it is another sign of Big Brother looking over their shoulders. Although the appropriate solution for this problem is not yet clear, managers must realize that encroaching on their subordinates' privacy has a profound impact on the psychological contract.

A Mutual Commitment to Support One Another's Needs During Times of Change

The third dimension has to do with a mutual agreement to support the other during times requiring significant change. The employee should understand that the organization must respond accurately to changing environmental demands. He cannot expect that the organization will maintain the status quo just to support his personal comfort level. The organization's mandated role is to continually adapt and evolve in relationship to the business environment, in order to support the shareholders, meet the needs of the customer, ward off the competition, and support the long-terms needs of its employees.

But at the same time, there needs to be an understanding by management that, as the organization changes and expects its people to change, the organization has a reciprocal obligation to support its people in addressing the change requirements. Says the employee, "If you want me to accept the changes, help me understand what's happened that forced this change, what alternatives you considered, why we'll be better off with this plan, and why we should see it as worthwhile to hang in there. If you also want me to put my heart in it and take personal ownership over the change, please acknowledge the toll it will have on us, provide us with the kinds of support we need to get ready for it, and give us as much control as possible over how it will be rolled out."

The psychological contract is a way of ensuring mutual and reciprocal trust and commitment. In solid psychological contracts, work provides people with meaning and purpose, the challenge and stimulation of purposeful activities, the support of others working on those activities, the potential of success, and the reward and "good feeling" of working well with others. Think of a psychological contract as the negotiation between two porcupines huddling together for warmth on a freezing winter night. The trick is for them to get close enough to share their body heat, without getting so close as to hurt each other.

A violated psychological contract can occur whenever there is a significant organizational change, whether the violation was intended or not. When people and their organization are in sync, even with tremendous workloads, people feel good about themselves and their companies. When the aspirations, values, and modes of behaving change, people not only experience loss but also a basic fracture of their sense of self and trust in the organizational relationship.

To forge a new psychological contract, managers need to know that this implicit psychological contract exists and remain aware of their peoples' unspoken—and often unconscious—expectations. They must be on the lookout for signs, such as betrayal, anger, hurt, and withdrawal, of a violated contract. It is critical that they acknowledge the altered contract and its impact on people. Then they need to put forth, in active two-way discussion, their new assumptions, new expectations of what can and cannot be negotiated, and what can and cannot be changed. In order to recover the trust and confidence of their people, managers must convince them that proceeding down this new path is good, is fair, and is the best way to ensure the employees' future success.

Within an Accountability Framework

Psychological contracts exist between all people who find themselves in some ongoing mutually dependent relationship. This is true between husbands and wives, parents and children, teachers and students, basketball teammates. It is also true in many kinds of work organizations other than managerial leadership systems. One can also identify psychological contracts in partnerships, in churches, in universities, and among medical staff members in a hospital. What is unique about the psychological contracts between managers and their subordinates is that they are influenced strongly by the accountability relationship that exists between them.

Managers are inescapably accountable for what their subordinates do, how well they do it, and whether or not they do it within defined boundaries. This is not true, for instance, between a managing partner of a law firm and another partner within the firm. Partners are the owners of the partnership; hence they are also its shareholders and members of its governing body. But the authority a managing partner has over any one partner is quite limited and principally consists of personal persuasion. She is elected by the partners and thus has political authority in relation to them, whereas a true manager (in a managerial hierarchy) is appointed into a role by his own manager, who then delegates authority to him over every subordinate and holds him accountable for those subordinates.

In Chapter 1, we talked about managerial authority and accountability and described the manager-subordinate relationship in a way that sounded quite a bit less personal than the discussion of the psychological contract previously described. This is one of the apparent paradoxes about the relationship. Although it is intimate (the psychological contract requires an accurate understanding of each subordinate as an individual), it's not personal. (Just ask the outspoken Mr. Petro!) A manager must accept that she is accountable for her people's effectiveness. If a subordinate can't carry his own weight in the role—even after proper coaching—she must remove him from the role. As Carlos de Leone said in *The Godfather,* "It ain't personal, Sonny, it's just business."

A Famine of Accountability

What happens when companies as a whole ignore the fact that they are accountability hierarchies? What type of engagement ensues when the accountabilities are not spelled out and managers attempt to engage their employees solely through "feeding their expressed needs?" In a 1997 article, *The Wall Street Journal* (*WSJ*) reported on the consequences of too much empowerment.[3]

The article explained that just a few years before, in 1994, Architectural Support Services Inc. (ASSI), a provider of computer-aided design services to architect clients, had been on top of the world. It had grown so successful so fast, in fact, that *Fortune* magazine had even run a cover story about it. Beneath the glossy, color cover photo, 10 of ASSI employees could be seen grinning, triumphant and proud. The *Fortune* caption trumpeted, "Where the employees take charge of their future."

But by the time *WSJ* ran its report only a scant few years later, ASSI's happy world had come crashing down. It was all a matter of "too much empowerment," *WSJ* pronounced, reporting that a mere one year later (in 1995) all but two of ASSI's employees had walked out on its owners, "embittered and divided against the very company that gave them control." Instead of enhancing commitment, this approach killed it. Despite such go-go clients as fast-rising star Home Depot, success just wouldn't stick. So what had gone so wrong?

Again, *WSJ*'s verdict was clear: "plenty of authority…too little accountability." In formulating ASSI's management policies, one of the partners "immersed herself in books, tapes and seminars that appealed to her sensibilities as a rebellious baby boomer. Teams. Empowerment. Profit sharing. No hierarchies." For a while, this seemed a decidedly winning approach as the company went on to earn much coverage in the business media and even as a textbook case of successful modern management in a newly published business compendium. But all the initial success failed to last.

Though ASSI's employees had free reign to schedule their own jobs and to implement them at their own pace, many also took umbrage whenever a company partner suggested they were behind in their schedules. Others chafed when a customer complained or made a special demand. Let a partner consider sending someone to a professional development program and the remark was typically viewed as a harsh criticism of that individual's capabilities. In general, the attitude of employees to managers at ASSI seemed to be, "Get out of my face!"

Can you see how such an organization, functioning without balanced levels of authority and accountability can ignore the intended results and prevent them from ever materializing at all? Sadly, business all over the world operates without this balance, short on common sense, mired in fantasy and stress, constantly running short of hoped-for potential and wished-for results. Worse, many managers today lack an awareness of any alternative. In their minds, traditional command and control vs. more recent empowerment represent the only two management options that exist.

At this point, you realize that they are not the only options. But how exactly does the QQT/R approach work in terms of precisely defining accountabilities (on both sides of the desk) in order to leverage and engage commitment?

Gaining Commitment

What differentiates accountability from responsibility is that with accountability commitments are made to others; with responsibility they are made to oneself. Commitments to others are obligations. QQT/Rs *are* commitments, and no surprises to the manager can be tolerated. When an employee commits to a QQT/R, she is obligated to deliver to her manager precisely that QQT/R—neither more nor less—unless the manager agrees to change it prior to the time of completion.

Now, under what conditions would any sensible employee make such a firm commitment? Why would he put his word and his future on the line with such a tough requirement to live up to? To begin, every employee must feel that communication up, across, and down the organization is open, frank, and fair. Denis Turcotte, EVP at Tembec, a fast-growing global wood products company, begins all discussions with his people with a reminder that he expects two-way, "full, true, and plain disclosure." Employees must not be afraid to speak directly and honestly with their managers when discussing context or when engaged in two-way planning. In particular, they must speak candidly, eyeball-to-eyeball, during the QQT/R definition process about what they believe is the most ambitious commitment they can make—and under what boundary conditions—and what commitments are just not possible. They must be prepared to explain why or why not but also to listen openly if their manager pushes back with a request for a more ambitious QQT/R, believing it is achievable.

Under no circumstances, however, should any employee commit to targets that he simply does not believe are possible. Doing so, in all likelihood, would require going back several times to his manager, attempting to renegotiate the QQT/R, and would leave the manager having to scramble again and again to reformulate her own plans for delivering on her own QQT/Rs. One key to engaging subordinate willingness to stretch themselves and commit to delivering on their QQT/Rs, therefore, is a frank and open dialogue in which everyone is kept honest.

Another key is for managers to actively engage their subordinates while formulating their own plans for meeting their QQT/Rs. Deciding on a plan is an essential part of the work of anyone carrying out an assignment. In the case of managers, developing their plans with their teams can be an important part of teamworking in order to provide opportunities for the involvement of subordinates. Against the background of a well-established context (much more about this in Chapter 5), a manager should present to subordinates, as early as possible, alternatives for how he or she is planning to proceed. Such a procedure allows the manager to get the benefit of subordinate inputs and to give subordinates the opportunity to provide such inputs. It should be made clear to subordinates that they are accountable for making their views available and for giving their managers their best advice.

There is no better way to build commitment from subordinates to support their manager's plan (to meet her QQT/Rs) than to create the opportunity for them to become actively involved in shaping that plan. When employees have helped to construct their manager's plan and have actively participated in defining their own QQT/Rs, they see their own imprint on the team's blueprint. Personal ownership is clearly the basis for commitment.

Managing for Fantasy: When Engagement Goes Awry

We have looked at two ways in which companies manage for fantasy. Both involve a misalignment between accountability and authority. The most commonly found are in organizations that delegate accountability without the requisite authority. As described in Chapter 1, these companies rely heavily on the strong sense of their employees' personal responsibility to fill in for the lack of "positional" authority and expect them to "work the system" somehow to get the job done. Getting results in this way usually comes out of peoples' hide (with conflict, overwork, cut corners, and so on) and almost always ends up sub-optimizing the whole in order to deliver on a particular task. After a while, most employees become weary and cynical about the unfairness and lack of reciprocity experienced in the psychological contract. One variation on this theme is seen in companies whose managers habitually force their subordinates to sign up for totally unrealistic targets (which nobody really believes in) and then choose to let it pass if the employees put up a good effort. I call these "superstretch goal-forgiveness systems."

The second variation of managing for fantasy was described earlier in this chapter, when people are empowered—that is, given authority but not held accountable. This usually results in people becoming quite self-absorbed (doing whatever they want to do) and entitled (feeling the company owes them the right to do whatever they want). I often refer to these as "empowerment-entitlement systems."

In neither case is the company able to accurately predict what it could produce nor is it able to reliably ensure that it will be produced. And in neither case does the company achieve the mature mutual and reciprocal commitment from its employees required to realize its full potential. They create, instead, disengagement.

A third example of companies that manage for fantasy is that of a "no excuses, unforgiving systems" approach to accountability. In this case, companies have usually obtained all the improvements they can through mechanistic and cost-cutting solutions and still find they are not consistently able to meet their targets. Having no clear understanding of the true nature of accountability, they resort to a meaner approach—namely "no excuses!" This is typically associated with a compensation system where pay is tied closely to countable outputs above or below the negotiated annual target.

If you recall the discussion about the difference between employees and subcontractors in Chapter 1, you will recognize that this approach begins to treat so-called employees more and more like contractors. The most natural response from the employee under these circumstances is to figure out how to protect himself and how to maximize his own earnings, because the company is seeking to put much of the risk on his shoulders. The first behavior we typically see is employees "sandbagging" their managers and "lowballing" their commitments, seeking wiggle room, because no excuses will be allowed. The second is creative, and often ruthless, gamesmanship with the goal of maximizing one's own outputs by year end in order to maximize one's pay. The third cost to the organization is the general unwillingness on the part of employees to make adjustments in their plans, which their managers or peers may seek due to changing conditions. Under such management approaches, maximizing one's own compensation replaces supporting the manager and the team as the objective.

	MANAGING FOR REALITY	MANAGING FOR FANTASY		
		1	2	3
SLOGAN	No surprises!	Superstretch!	Empowerment!	No excuses!
POSTURE	Accountability	Forgiveness	Entitlement	Fear
GOALS	Ambitious, but realistic	Impossible	Self-defined	Padded
CULTURE	Tough, but fair	Unrealistic, but forgiving	Totally forgiving	Unrealistic and unforgiving
ADAPTABILITY	Flexible and disciplined	Flexible and undisciplined	Totally undisciplined	Inflexible and disciplined
DRIVING FORCE	Accountability and responsibility	Mainly responsibility	Responsibility and self-indulgence	Survival of the fittest
ENGAGEMENT	Commitments	Obedience	Guilt	Controls
INTEGRITY	Honest and direct	Manipulative and indirect	Shamelessly manipulative	Manipulative and deceptive
COMMUNICATION	Two-way, open	Partial two-way, guarded	Cliches: "Do the right thing"	Top-down, closed
PRIMARY CONCERN	Organization first, then me	Me first, then organization	Me, although I say it's you	Me
MOTIVATION	Pride and respect	Excitement vs. loyalty	Do your own thing!	Fear and survival
APPROACH TO WORK PROBLEMS	Cooperation	Compromise	Calloused	Conflict
TEAMWORKING	Strong	Variable	With like-minded people	Every person for himself
APPRAISAL and PAY	Effectiveness within limits	Performance	Effort	Outputs

Engagement is neither a single act nor a simple set of actions. It is about setting in place an overall approach to managerial leadership, based on LEAD. It has, at its core, a basic respect for human capability, responsibility, and accountability and seeks to find a common ground, based on common value, as the basis for working hard and well together. The table above illustrates the characteristics of an accountability system that manages for reality and contrasts them with the three types of fantasy-management approaches.

Managing for Reality: Engaged at Last!

We now have most of the basic building blocks of engagement in place. Employment is not an entitlement; it is a privilege. It is an opportunity for people to gain a greater measure of security than they would have if working for themselves as entrepreneurs. They have guaranteed salary, benefits, and opportunities to be challenged, to master, to grow. In return, they must commit to add value to the organization at a level consistent with the size of role they are given, and to honor their commitments, with no surprises. They must continually earn the right to remain in role—even to remain employed. It is a simple, mature accountability contract.

In addition, their managers understand that people will fully invest themselves, and their capabilities, only when they see they can do good work, receive fair recognition for it, and develop their full potential. This then becomes the basis for negotiating a mature psychological contract.

Thus, there are four sets of working conditions that, if fully achieved, will ensure the full engagement of employee commitment to support the organization in succeeding:

1. Personal security.
2. Personal value.

3. Effective leadership.
4. A culture of fairness.

Personal Security

If the number-one concern of the employing company was anything other than providing a safe and healthy working environment for its employees, wouldn't you expect those employees to feel that they are expendable commodities? A somewhat disgruntled employee might think, "If you don't value my need to stay healthy, support my family, and continue to grow with the company, I guess I'll need to hold back some and look out for myself." Similarly, if the company appears to make only expedient decisions (rather than well-conceived ones), not designed to ensure the long-term health and perpetuation of the organization, employees should rightly question whether they want to invest their mental capital and their career aspirations there. The employee concludes, "If I want a secure future for myself and my family, I better look elsewhere."

Personal Value

Because employees spend more than half of their waking hours in the workplace, they would naturally prefer to work in roles and on assignments that have some personal meaning—roles and assignments, that is, that they consider on some level to be valuable work. In addition, people want to be challenged, to test and apply their capabilities. They want work that is sufficiently complex that they can sink their teeth into it and really add value when they solve its problems. Nothing disengages people more quickly than giving them boring QQT/Rs that have far less impact on the organization than they are capable of providing.

Employees know when they are not realizing their full potential. They become frustrated when they're not able to give the kinds of results and add the kinds of value that they know they're capable of. It makes plain sense to them that the organization would want their managers to work with them to identify areas that, if developed, could help them realize this potential. People want to know where they stand, both in their current role and in their career possibilities. Employees become significantly more engaged with their company when their managers work with them to enhance their effectiveness and develop their capabilities to permit them to be promoted throughout their career in ways that are consistent with the maturation of their potential.[4]

Finally, people receive significant value from having mature, constructive working relationships with others at work. Employees value working effectively with others to produce spectacular results and create a winning team. Their sense of self-worth grows significantly when they have given and received meaningful help to and from others. When the organization manages for fantasy, however, it pits people against each other. When the organization fails to clarify who is accountable for what, in relationship to whom, it ensures unproductive conflict and strain between well-intentioned, responsible people. To ensure engagement not only upwards, but with others across the organization, leaders need to get accountabilities clear, align accountabilities with authorities, and set the context within which people know how to best support each other.

Effective Leadership

People want information and meaningful control over their lives. Good managers engage their people around open and direct discussions. What is the organization up against? What is the unit up against? What are the manager and the team up against? The most effective managers create opportunities for employee input into the plan of attack on those realities, and respond respectfully to those inputs. Those that should be incorporated are integrated, and with appropriate recognition. Those that cannot be incorporated likewise obligate the manager to explain why, providing an opportunity to further coach and develop subordinates. In this way, employees have direct understanding of what they're up against, including immediate and recognizable input into what needs to be done to meet the challenge.

Above all, employees want to succeed. They want challenging QQT/Rs, but they also want to have the resources and capable processes that are necessary in order to succeed. Being "set up to fail" repeatedly breeds cynicism and disengagement.

Finally, people want recognition for their contributions, both public and private. Nothing turns off an employee quicker than a manager who hogs the "organizational limelight" for himself, taking credit for his own subordinates' good work. Though the most direct form of recognition is compensation, many employees today are extremely cynical about the manner in which their companies reward them. My own experience is that people will view compensation as equitable if it can meet three criteria:

1. Range of pay is tied directly to an objective measure of the sizes of roles.
2. The pay step within such range is tied to a fair appraisal of the overall value an employee has contributed.
3. Actual pay (base plus merit) is determined by the manager's assessment of his employee's unique efforts and contributions throughout the year.[5]

Employees always experience pay as equitable or fair whenever it is seen as reasonable in relation to what others are compensated. When people feel they have fairly earned and been fairly compensated for what they make, they trust the organization and become even more engaged.

A Culture of Fairness

This brings us back to the essence of the psychological contract, namely fairness, trust, respect, and reciprocity. People will never fully commit or sign on when they perceive their work relationship as unjust—and not just when they themselves are treated unfairly, either. Consider how many organizational change efforts have stalled when the employees who survived the cuts feel that those who didn't were treated badly? Most think, "If management can do this to *them,* why should I feel secure they won't do it to *me* next time?" Engagement, after all, is all about entrusting your fate, to some degree, to others so that all your creative efforts can be dedicated toward helping these others succeed.

Alignment

In Chapter 3, we explored the nature of complexity in managerial systems and how leaders must leverage the judgments of many people in order to meet their goals. In this chapter, we discussed the conditions necessary to engage the full, enthusiastic commitment of employees to apply that judgment within an accountability framework. In Chapter 5, we will delve into concepts and techniques for managers to align that judgment (and exercise of discretion) in order to ensure an optimal, orchestrated implementation of their strategies.

---

[1]This theme (that everyone has a powerful need to do socially valued work) is one that Elliott Jaques first argued systematically in *Equitable Payment* and set out in *Requisite Organization,* p. 14.

[2]Levinson (with Charlton R. Price, Kenneth J. Munden, Harold J. Mandl, and Charles M. Solley), *Men, Management, and Mental Health,* p. 22.

[3] Thomas Petzinger, Jr., "The Front Lines," *Wall Street Journal,* 11 April, 1997.

[4]The preceding arguments have been strongly put forward by Elliott Jaques, op. cit.

[5]Jaques set forth his findings on felt-fair differential pay and differentials in level of work in *Measurement of Responsibility.*

Chapter 5

Aligning Judgment

What on earth were they thinking? After a minor business mistake or a company-wide disaster, managers usually ask this question of their subordinates. Similarly, subordinates will likely toss the same question around to each other about management. It is human nature to second-guess. However, the need for second-guessing could be eliminated entirely if managers and subordinates clearly communicated their intentions at the beginning of a project.

In this chapter, you'll explore how you, as a manager, might convey your thinking, intentions, and even your wishes to subordinates before an assignment begins, in ways that minimize the probability of difficulties and maximize a project's chances of success. As I noted back in Chapter 2, management's thinking and intentions together comprise the context in which subordinates should be operating. If such context is regularly and widely communicated, the result will be genuine alignment within and throughout the organization.

The Rocky Road to Alignment

Alignment has become a popular goal, or at least a popular buzzword, in business recently. Many managers are finding themselves in the midst of the rubble of such noble experiments as employee-empowerment and self-directed teams. The difficulty is that empowering people to do what they think is best, or encouraging leaderless teams to direct themselves, throws an organization out of alignment just as surely as driving your car directly into a large pothole will throw its wheels out of alignment.

Lack of alignment in an organization creates confusion regarding overarching goals, lack of focus on QQT/Rs, disconnects between goals and actions, misdirected or conflicting efforts, and other conditions sure to suboptimize organizational performance. Such suboptimization translates into other negative effects: lower revenues and earnings, missed opportunities, and greater chances for unnecessary and potentially costly risk-taking.

In contrast, proper alignment leads to the clarification of overarching goals, the intensification of subordinates' focus on QQT/Rs, the establishment of effective links between goals and actions, and the coordination of everyone's efforts. All this enables the company to keep improving its financial performance, to capitalize on opportunities as they present themselves, and to mitigate unnecessary risk.

Before attempting to develop alignment in your own environment, however, let's first define it. Sadly, this is something many managers never bother to or don't know how to do. They may think in terms of aligning people toward a specific goal, say, increasing sales, cutting costs, or getting a certain product developed. I would admit that's better than nothing. But we have found that for truly spectacular results, it is far better to aim higher, seeking alignment of thinking in broader and more productive ways.

Context: A Manager's Secret Weapon

We begin to create alignment when we convey our thinking to our subordinates. More specifically, we must also convey our plans, which is to say our QQT/Rs and the means we imagine of attaining them.

Even seemingly obvious intentions should be carefully explained. Instead of simply declaring "cut costs," it is far better to say, "We've got to cut our costs by 15 percent because they are so out of line with those of our competitors. Only by pricing ourselves 8- to 10-percent lower will we be able to win back much of the business we have recently lost to our lower-priced competition."

By giving subordinates more than just the most rudimentary facts, we help them understand our goals as well as the motivation behind those goals. By informing them and taking them into our confidence, we make them our allies and partners. To do otherwise is to treat subordinates like serfs and drones— not a smart way, obviously, to develop employees who give a damn. Setting context allows—and obligates—subordinates to take your intentions into account as they plan and implement their own accountabilities.

Conveying your intentions in detail enables your people to better understand and more accurately address the many competing demands they will face and the tradeoffs they will have to make later on. For example, you wouldn't want your salespeople to lower prices to the point where you couldn't afford to deliver quality products and good service and still meet your business objectives. Your people should have a sense of what they're going to be up against—in the larger picture— so that all the ramifications of context can be reliably anticipated and prepared for.

To do it right, then, managers must learn ways to communicate, and interpret, complexity. To add real value, this means no more mere barking of orders or simplistic statements. "Go cut costs over at human resources" and "I want you to

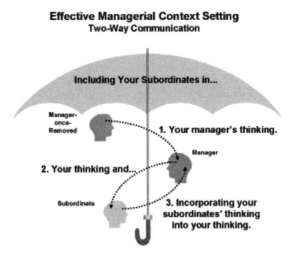

Effective Managerial Context Setting
Two-Way Communication

Including Your Subordinates in...

Manager-once-Removed

1. Your manager's thinking.

Manager

2. Your thinking and...

Subordinate

3. Incorporating your subordinates' thinking into your thinking.

handle the Jennings account and make sure we come out with a profit" are such context-less QQT/Rs that leave too much to the subordinates' imaginations without a clue as to how their own actions need to fit into the organization's larger picture.

The requirements of good managerial leadership begin with every manager at every level including their subordinates in two levels of management thinking (above them) and then incorporating the best ideas of those subordinates into their own. As the graphic above illustrates, the setting of context requires the active translation of the complexity from each level into a useful form for subordinates. The purposes are to better orient subordinates as to how their QQT/Rs fit into the bigger picture and to inform them about the types of tradeoffs that may need to be made. When well communicated, context allows subordinates to "think smarter" when constructing and adjusting plans to deliver their QQT/Rs in a way that most closely supports the original intentions behind those assignments. When context is not communicated well, it can make for quite a mess.

OTC (Off-Track Context)

Lorie Adamson, a new senior VP of manufacturing at a biotech firm, made the decision that her division had to begin cutting lots of expenses...and fast. What she didn't clearly communicate, however, was how or why it should be done.

Lorie's subordinates *assumed* they knew what she meant. She, meanwhile, assumed that they knew what she meant. However, some months later problems arose when it became clear there had never been any such alignment of understanding.

Lorie's order had come down in such a simplified fashion. "Cut costs, NOW!" she thundered. Her staff assumed that what she meant was just that and only that. Cut, cut, cut everywhere they could. Cut costs to the bone. Spare nothing.

But Lorie had meant something quite different—namely, to cut where possible but to keep costs up at some minimally acceptable level. Don't let things slide or interfere with prudent manufacturing practices. And certainly don't stop planning and investing for the future. If a machine had to be replaced because of failing production capacity, replace it. If walls needed to be painted to ensure a clean working environment, call painters in. Maintain adequate supply inventories. Keep employing capable and experienced people. Lorie's *unarticulated* intentions were to cut expenses in a sustainable way.

By the time Lorie got around to reviewing what had been done, the division looked very different. Some machines were now running well below capacity with second-rate parts. Cleaning crews had been cut back to twice a week rather than every day. Door handles and windowpanes were missing but never replaced. One afternoon, Lorie was giving a tour of the main manufacturing facility to a group of European investors. "What's going on here?" Lorie cried out, much to the dismay of her employees.

"You wanted us to cut costs, so we did!" they explained afterwards. "We've slashed our budgets to the bone, just as you asked us to."

With no context given and no guidelines, the true aims of this VP could not be acted upon. This also placed in jeopardy the intentions of Lorie's manager, the company CEO. Obviously, any hope the organization had of coordinating its overall vision had been dashed, at least temporarily. And short of adopting a rigorous practice of context setting, the firm's troubles were just beginning.

Beating "The Dog Ate My Homework" Syndrome

Hearing about the concept of context setting, learning how it works, and going out and practicing it, day in and day out, strikes many managers as an impossible and, in some ways, less-than-worthwhile journey. Resistance to substantive context setting runs high in the minds of many managers. And most of the excuses can be can be captured under one or more of the following three headings:

- "I'm too busy."
- "They don't need to know."
- "They won't care. And they probably wouldn't understand anyway."

"I'm too busy."

Though it doesn't have to be, context-setting, especially when a part of the QQT/R-defining process, can appear at first glance to be quite time consuming.

Because everyone is so overworked these days, it is easy for many employees to react to this unfamiliar requirement as if it were the last straw, the additional chore that will finally do them in.

Truth be told, the learning curve can sometimes be great. A company that supplies glass to the automotive industry was in the throes of converting to the accountability leadership cornerstone. At first, managers there complained loudly that setting context was "a waste of time" and "hugely burdensome." The reason? Context-setting requires a new approach to delegation itself.

How often have you heard managers say (or said yourself), "It would be a lot easier, and faster, to just do this myself than to delegate it. I'd probably get it done right and quicker than my subordinate could do it"? Logically we know that when the QQT/R is of appropriate size to delegate, in the long run it makes sense to do so. If the manager keeps everything in her own task basket, she'd be left with no time to work on the more complex tasks, those she cannot delegate. Setting context is the primary means by which savvy managers help their subordinates to think and act smart when planning for, and implementing, those delegated QQT/Rs.

In the end, however, the glass manufacturer reaped enormous benefits from context-setting. At a staff meeting I sat in on, the CEO said to his senior team, "It may sound hackneyed, but we have to spend money to make money. Similarly, we need to spend time setting context in order to save time and money and improve productivity in the long run."

"They don't need to know."

Many managers feel that their subordinates don't need to know all the details or that they should be able to just do what they're told with just the bare facts. This may be true for simple and repetitive assignments. However, this "keep 'em in the dark" practice can get in the way of aligning the thinking, decisions, and coordinated actions of multiple subordinates around complex assignments under rapidly changing conditions.

The difficulty in setting meaningful context arises when a manager tries to consider all of the variables that could have an impact on the delegated QQT/R. Which ones of those does the subordinate already understand well?

Which ones does he know something about? Which important ones might not even show up on the subordinate's radar screen? This problem deepens if the manager were to ask himself, "What option would I choose if this or that condition arose?" and then tried to figure out, "Why that choice and not one of three others that could also apply?"

The underlying issue is that managers are rarely cognizant of all the factors they consider when making a decision or of many of the underlying principles and assumptions they apply in arriving at that decision. It takes real mental effort, concentration, and two-way communication with others to extract this understanding from the manager's mind. Given this, how is that manager's subordinate going to be aware of all the subtle nuances that go into making optimal decisions about his delegated QQT/R if the manager himself has trouble articulating them in the first place? He cannot know—unless he's a mind reader (not likely) or his manager has taken the time and effort to set context.

Phil Baker, one of our clients, tells us that he has come to a point of assuming his subordinates know nothing about the context surrounding a new QQT/R. "I give all my guys license to stop me in my tracks if I'm not giving them the very best overview," Phil proudly says. "I often shortchange the context without intending to, particularly when I am extremely familiar with the topic. It feels kind of unnatural for me to weave this complex web of interconnections when it is all so intuitively obvious to me. Sometimes I even wonder if I'm going too far, but mostly that's a result of feeling way too busy. In fact, my team ends up needing less and less context as time goes on, when I set the proper level of context at the beginning. They now know how I think and often correctly anticipate my decisions before I make them. This has really freed me up to leave them alone to resolve problems between them. [More than] 90 percent of the time, they choose the same internal adjustments I would have made if they had come to me."

Phil tells a story of assigning to Kevin McHenry, his VP of business planning, the QQT/R to "develop some alternatives for driving our energy costs down." His suggestion was to look at the merits of putting up a power co-generation facility. This required the VP to compare and contrast the cost of constructing it internally with the cost of subcontracting it out. Within traditional delegation, that might be all that would be said. "Go out and see what you find" would typically be the way this kind of conversation came to a close.

But after implementing the LEAD approach, Phil realized that such a terse delegation style left these kinds of assignments vulnerable to misinterpretation and inadequate results. "This could end up being anywhere from a $25 million to a $100 million project," Phil explains. "Depending on how Kevin went about researching it, and what he looked for within the research, it could take off in many different directions. Given that, I knew I would be saving grief in the long run by taking more than 30 seconds to lay out the assignment to my guy. Exploring the assignment in more depth would help bring it to a more successful conclusion, with far less rework and fewer detours."

"They won't care. And they probably wouldn't understand anyway."

This theme reveals two serious problems. The first is not appreciating the importance of leveraging judgment. It is precisely through setting context and giving subordinates a broader, more substantial framework within which to exercise judgment that managers add value. If managers do not believe that their subordinates are capable of understanding the context, then either the subordinates don't have enough horsepower (which reflects badly on the manager's selections) or the managers are not able to translate the complexities effectively. In either case, leverage is not being achieved.

The second problem goes to the heart of managerial engagement, the key to enlisting and harnessing employee commitment. Once again, it is through the active, two-way setting of context, clarifying the importance of the subordinate's QQT/Rs in supporting the big picture,[1] that managers demonstrate how much they value their subordinates' work. Failing to set context, incorporating subordinate input into the manager's thinking, creates a self-fulfilling prophecy. If you treat your people as though they shouldn't care and their input doesn't matter, they won't care!

And when managers seek to incorporate subordinate input into their own thinking and planning, they not only reinforce the value of the subordinate, but they also construct more complete plans that reflect subordinate creativity. They think of plans as theirs, not just the manager's. Their people become involved; they buy into the big picture. They invest themselves in the team's outcome. They begin working *with* the manager, not just *for* her—and certainly not *against* her.

Another client, Dick Fleming, the CEO of a division within a high-tech company well-known for its cutting-edge R&D, got a hard lesson about not setting context. After attending one of our seminars on accountable leadership, he sought to restart a stalled corporate initiative he began six months earlier. He had delegated to Claire Voight, his VP of process development, the task of leading an organization-wide project involving the cultivation of 30 to 50 "communities of practice" within a two-year time span. Such communities, it was hoped, would provide a basis for continuous and seamless knowledge-sharing within the company.

Claire assumed that the CEO wanted the same disciplined approach she normally undertook when reengineering major processes. Claire's team had produced a "grand, mechanical, rigid process for creating communities," Dick later thought, that was "missing the real point that communities get born and grow spontaneously and naturally. They can be nourished, but they probably cannot be 'instituted,' especially by a fixed, repetitive process." Basically, the study team had defaulted to the kind of process they knew so well—that is, how to craft very detailed operational plans. Dick ended up with a blow-by-blow procedural document with a two-year endpoint. What Dick had envisioned was an initial three-month experiment, something through which the company could learn how to build communities.

By this time, it was obvious: Dick had simply not set context as well as he should have for Claire and her team. True, he had communicated his wish for this project to evolve into a new way of life for his organization, imagining that it would probably take a time period of about two years. But he hadn't thought through what could and should happen *within* those two years, what could go wrong, and what could go right. He hadn't clarified his own hopes for the initiative, why he cared so much, and why everyone else should care, too.

So Dick sat down with the team and said, "Look, never mind about the two-year plan, forget about this as a step-by-step project. Let's just talk about now, and how, in three months, we need to have one prototype experiment successfully started around a particular community of practice. Now, you guys help me understand how we get there. And why it might matter to you, to me, to everyone."

By allowing his team to be a real partner in the understanding and defining of the assignment, sharing all of his thinking, including his own aspirations, Dick provided them with the opportunity to genuinely care about the whole assignment.

As you might imagine, the response from Claire's team was phenomenal. Quickly, team members located a methodology that could be brought in to help them develop their first community as the whole operation shifted. "Let's do this experiment, Claire, and not worry about the next step yet," Dick said. "I'm confident that once you understand the nature of the beast, you and the others be able to construct the necessary steps to get where we all need to be in two years."

Easy as Why (and What and How)

We have looked at some managers who resisted setting context as well as the consequences of their resistance. As they discovered, setting context does require time, careful thought, and a willingness to paint a picture together with their subordinates. But, as they found, setting context is worth it.

Managers who need to be omnipotent feel they must appear to their subordinates to be fully in control. These managers need to relax. They must let the two-way discussion of context build and grow, as new insights are generated and tested and old assumptions are discarded and replaced. Above all, managers need to be receptive to questions—even outright challenges—from their subordinates in order to make sure that everyone has the most

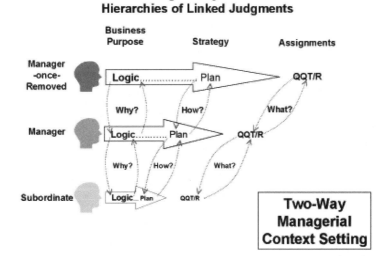

Managerial Systems:
Hierarchies of Linked Judgments

complete and accurate understanding of the big picture. The key is to build a logical sequence of what, how, and why.

In the beginning, there was the goal and the plan. For the shareholders, the plan is the long-range strategy to meet their long-term objectives. It is formulated by the CEO and ratified by the board of directors. But the long-range strategy is itself a framework within which each of the CEO's subordinate executives must construct *their* plans to meet *their* delegated QQT/Rs. And their plans, in turn, provide a framework for their own subordinates, within which they must develop their plans for meeting their accountabilities.

Every manager at every level has in mind a rationale for why he is constructing his plans as he does. This logic is important for the manager's subordinates to understand, as well, because they need to align their thinking along the same lines. I refer to this logic as the "why" a manager designs a plan the way she does. I refer to the plan as the "how" she intends to accomplish the QQT/R. And I refer to the QQT/R itself as the "what" she is accountable for delivering.

The Context-Setting Linchpin

The goal of alignment is to ensure that every employee has an accurate understanding of how his assignments fit into the next two levels up and across the organization. The immediate manager must be accountable for setting that context—and for doing so at a level of complexity appropriate to that employee. Let's think of the context-setting manager as the linchpin who connects the level above with the level below.

The Big Picture *(Context: Two Levels Up)*

As the preceding Managerial Context-Setting graphic summarizes, Manager B begins by describing her manager's (Manager A's) task basket: "This is *what* my manager was assigned by his manager, this is *how* my manager is planning to meet that accountability, and this is *why* he chose to do it that way." Of course, the context-setting manager (Manager B) was included in her manager's context and even contributed to his ideas about how to meet his accountabilities. This allows Manager B to be plugged into and fully knowledgeable about her manager's thinking. We call this context, two levels up from Subordinate C, *the big picture.*

The Immediate Picture *(Context: One Level Up)*

Next, Manager B describes what is in her own task basket: "This is *what* my manager (Manager A) delegated to me. Can you see that my QQT/R is a step of his plan? My current thinking about *how* I will get it done is as follows, but I won't decide on a plan until I get your input. This is my logic for considering *why* each of these approaches might have merit. You can see how they are aligned with *my* manager's thinking." We call this context, one level up from Subordinate C, *the immediate picture.*

At this point, the manager has successfully presented the *upward context.* Subordinate C knows how his QQTRs fit into the greater organizational universe.

Input Advice *(Two-Way-Context Definition)*

Next, Manager B seeks *input advice* from Subordinate C: "Given the picture I have presented, *what* insights or suggestions can you give me from where you sit? *How* can I improve my plan? *Why* do I need to consider additional factors before deciding on my plan?" This input not only strengthens Manager B's understanding of the opportunities and obstacles to be addressed, but it also allows *each* of her Subordinates C to contribute to, and feel greater ownership over, *her* plan. In effect, it becomes *their* plan.

QQT/R Definition *(Two-Way-Assignment Definition)*

The next step is an iterative, two-way manager-subordinate discussion, leading to the *definition of the subordinate's QQT/R.* Manager B's discourse to Subordinate C goes something like this: "Given my plan for achieving my QQT/R (which you helped me design), recommend to me the most ambitious QQT/R you could commit to (given everything else that is currently in your task basket) that would effectively support my plan. Ideally, you'll need minimal additional resources, because you'll find a way to spread out your existing

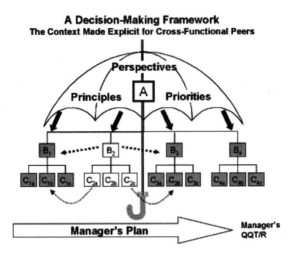

A Decision-Making Framework
The Context Made Explicit for Cross-Functional Peers

resources. However, if you need more than I can get for you, then recommend to me exactly how I should redefine your existing accountabilities to free up resources for this new assignment. Remember that you are still accountable for everything you've already committed to unless I agree to change them. So make sure you can deliver the entire task basket!"

Teamworking Context *(One-Level-Downward Context)*

Finally, how do Subordinate C_1's QQT/Rs fit into those of his teammates (C_2, C_3, C_4, etc.)? Once Manager B agrees to delegate an ambitious, yet realistic, QQT/R that Subordinate C_1 commits to deliver, then Manager B needs to set the *teamworking context.* Manager B says to *all* her Subordinate Cs: "This is how each of your accountabilities need to support mine. These are the principles governing how each of you must actively support each other, adjusting your plans together, in order to best support my optimal outcome, as long as each of you can still meet your individual accountabilities." This *downward context* is often difficult for managers to describe, because so much of their thinking about desirable subordinate interactions only comes to the surface when problems arise.

Decision-Making Frameworks *(Three-Level Detailing of Context)*

One way for managers, with their subordinates' help, to clarify their own thinking about these interactions is by engaging in scenario-planning with the team: "Now, if this sort of conflict were to occur, I would probably consider three or four options. I would then weigh each one against these five or six criteria. If the whole picture weighed more heavily in this direction, I would probably choose Option #1; if it weighed in this other direction, I would probably choose Option #2."

As the manager and subordinates continue to probe each other's reasoning and construct new scenarios, they begin to develop a reliable structure of perspectives and priorities. When fully explored, this becomes a formal *decision-making framework,* as depicted in the preceding graphic, within which all subordinates (and their subordinates) must come together to design, understand, and agree on solutions whenever there are new difficulties, dangers, or opportunities.

Alignment Achieved!

As we've seen in this chapter, alignment of thinking is as important for relative accountabilities as holding subordinates accountable for delivering on their commitments is for fixed accountabilities. But even if managers do both of these, what's to ensure that employees will act within the intended alignments—within the decision-making frameworks? It is one thing to measure whether subordinates deliver their QQT/Rs as defined and adhere to the defined policy and process limits. It is quite another to hold members of a team individually accountable for such intangibles as "coming together to design and agree on integrative solutions, whenever there are problems or opportunities between them." How in the world can a manager measure that?

The bad news is that you cannot measure it. The good news is that, as a manager, you *know*—or at least you should know—if your subordinate has gone out of his way to bring the whole team together to deliver the desired overall result—even when it made the job more difficult for his own unit. Managers are accountable for being close enough to their subordinates to observe and learn about their interactions with teammates and their creativity in conserving and improving resources, and in overcoming obstacles to delivering on their QQT/Rs. You cannot quantify these kinds of employee judgments, but you can accurately assess whether they are making good judgments when juggling the complex and ever-changing accountabilities in their task baskets.

The fundamentals of aligning judgment—from transforming intentions and wishes into managerial realities—are:

1. Establishing clear role accountabilities, matched with the corresponding authorities.
2. Setting clear and effective two-way context.
3. Defining, in two-way discussion, ambitious and achievable QQT/Rs.
4. Maintaining clear teamworking context and decision-making frameworks.

5.   Assessing employee effectiveness in making adjustments to support the contexts while still meeting their QQT/Rs.

We now have covered three of the four elements of accountability leadership: leveraging potential (L) in chapter 3; engaging commitment (E) in Chapter 4; and aligning judgment (A) in this chapter. In Chapter 6, I'll discuss the key concepts and applications necessary for developing capabilities (D).

---

[1] Elliott Jaques, *Requisite Organization,* p. 101.

Chapter 6
Developing Capabilities

We began this book by asking you how much of your company's potential is currently being realized. We defined that potential by asking you to imagine every resource (people, processes, technologies, assets, and so forth) being fully developed, every role being effectively filled with fully engaged people, and all structures and processes being perfectly aligned (so no energy is lost working the system). In hundreds of companies, on every populated continent, I hear the same answer from employees at every level: Barely one third of our potential is being realized and, therefore, leveraged. In this chapter, you'll explore the leadership role in developing capabilities to help employees realize their full potential.

A Terrible Thing to Waste

We want to begin by asking what is meant by *potential*[1] and how it differs from *performance*. You are all familiar with the expressions "he's just not working at his potential," and "she has the potential to handle a much bigger job," and "I think his career potential is enormous." What exactly do we mean by potential when used in these ways? And how exactly do we know or sense what a person's potential is, anyway? Where does the potential come from? Can we accurately measure it, the way we can height and blood pressure? Can you modify your potential with education, with will power, or with Prozac? Is it static or does it change over time? Is it innate or can it be acquired?

These questions may border on the ridiculous, but they are very important to the whole notion of leadership as leverage.

Potential by itself is useless. Unrealized potential is like a finely tuned Ferrari stuck in a showroom during a recession; the thwarted sports car never gets a chance to go from zero to 60 in 5.7 seconds. Similarly, having great potential year after year is what gets professional football coaches fired. The real measure of a coach's effectiveness is whether he can consistently deliver the performance from his players each season, win 12 or 14 games, and make the playoffs. Leadership is the catalyst or kinetic energy for leveraging potential. What companies actually hire people for is not potential, but performance.

Then what exactly is performance? High performance is what we need—and what we should be paying for—to get results today, referring to employees who, month after month, deliver high levels of value in their current positions. It may (or may not) apply to people who are also working at or near their full potential.

As with accountability, performance is a word that means different things in different companies. In some, it refers to those people who consistently deliver greater individual outputs. In others, it refers to people who are politically astute at working the system. I believe having the concepts of fixed and relative accountabilities allows us to be much more precise and have a commonly understood meaning. When everyone is obligated to deliver *precisely* the QQT/R he last agreed on with his manager, the only variables to assess become how *effectively* he delivered on his *relative* accountabilities. Thus, we will stop referring to performance at this point and, instead, talk about an individual's "effectiveness" in role.[2]

Effectiveness: An Exercise in Discretion

Let's revisit the fixed and relative accountabilities outlined in Chapter 1, using the metaphor of linked chains. Unlike gears, each link has some discretion about how to move in relation to those above and below, but always within defined boundaries. The metal, which binds the links together, is the equivalent of the QQT/Rs and the limits. If the metal is somehow compromised or broken, then the entire accountability chain falls apart.

As you'll recall, the *fixed* accountabilities can be summarized as follows:

1. A commitment to deliver a QQT/R is an obligation, not just a good intention. Unless an employee gets a manager to agree to change it—well in advance of its completion date—the employee is still responsible.

2. The defined policies, practices, rules, and regulations all apply. Employees do not get to choose, on their own, which ones they'll adhere to and which ones they'll ignore.

But it is meeting their *relative* accountabilities—by applying judgment in order to add maximum value to the organization—that require employees to exercise discretion. Over the years, I've identified four ways in which each employee can add considerable value to his role:

1. By committing to the most ambitious, yet achievable, QQT/Rs in the first place.
2. By delivering QQT/Rs which are the best fit for the purpose for which they were assigned.
3. By optimizing delegated resources, wherever possible, by conserving their use or by inventing ways to improve their efficiency (process improvement).
4. By adjusting one's own plans continually in relation to teammates and cross-functional peers so as to achieve the overall benefit for the company.

Here are the same four managerial exhortations articulated in 21st-century vernacular:

1. Don't play it safe. Commit aggressively, but honestly. I need your best and smartest shot, not your safest!
2. Work smart. Don't just get it done. Instead, always think about the larger plan your QQT/R is a part of and work toward making the larger plan succeed.
3. Act like the resources I delegate to you are yours. Constantly look to conserving them (increase profits today) and improving them (increase profits tomorrow).
4. Let's make sure we all understand how each of our individual accountabilities are intended to come together and then make whatever adjustments you can to support the whole, and still deliver your QQT/Rs—even if it makes the job more difficult for you and your people. Teamwork, teamwork, teamwork! That's what teamwork is all about.

How well an employee delivers on these relative accountabilities (while meeting his fixed accountabilities) is his overall "effectiveness" quotient. It represents the value an individual contributes to the organization. The more value an individual contributes, the higher the effectiveness appraisal and the more the organization will want to compensate him. The more value an employee contributes, the more secure his job and career in the company will be.

Conversely, someone who is not consistently able to deliver the minimum level of value required by a role and doesn't show signs, with appropriate coaching and development, of improving soon cannot be allowed to remain in the role. I'm not saying he should be fired. Remember Ed, the ad agency vice president who was unable to put together a coherent plan? As Ed was, the individual might be quite effective in another role. But it is his manager who is accountable for removing him from the role and replacing him with someone who is likely to be more effective. Remember: It's not personal; it's business!

Potential to Do *What*?

We now know what we mean by effectiveness. So, what then do we mean by potential? Simply stated, we mean that someone has the *possibility* of being effective in a role of a certain size if certain other conditions are met. We are making a judgment as to what level of work complexity someone *could* handle, if he had some additional capabilities that he could acquire. Potential is a hypothetical. Until Dr. Jaques came along, we were unclear as to what kind of capability it reflected and what created that capability in the first place.

Potential is an indirect assessment of the type and level of judgment a person possesses. By judgment, I mean exactly what was described in Chapter 3—namely, the capacity to handle complexity in order to solve problems. Bigger roles are more complex and require the people in them to be able to deal effectively with commensurate complexities. When we describe someone's current potential, we are trying to convey our impression of his horsepower, bandwidth, processing speed, or raw intelligence. When we ask whether we think someone is "big enough" for a role, we are trying to picture whether the individual is simply bright enough to handle the kinds of complexities found in that role. If he is big enough, we can then consider whether he also knows enough, cares enough, and is mature enough to succeed. But if he isn't currently processing at the level the role requires, he just doesn't have the potential to be effective in the role today. This is what we mean by *current potential.*

Potential: Here Today, Where Tomorrow?

Until now, I have kept our focus on assessing employees now. "What level of effectiveness does this individual currently demonstrate in her role?" a manager asks. "How large a role does she have the current potential to handle, if she were to acquire the skilled knowledge needed and were fully committed?" But is a person's potential static? Is it fixed for all time? These questions highlight another source of confusion in most organizations that try to track and develop their high-potential people. They usually mean "future" when they talk about "potential." A manager *should* ask, "How big a role does she have the potential to handle by the end of her career? Does she have what it takes to become CEO some day?"

Once again, Dr. Jaques to the rescue! He noticed back in the 1950s,[3] when he first discovered the underlying structure of levels of complexity, that when he plotted people's career paths over time, there was a trend towards predictable patterns of progression. Those who were in bigger roles when they were younger tended to advance more quickly in their careers. Was it just chance? Was it alchemy? Or was it a self-fulfilling prophecy?

To test for this type of bias in the actual role-selection decisions, Jaques decided to plot the assessment of people's current potential over time rather than their actual career path. To get at current potential, he asked the kinds of questions enumerated in this section's first paragraph and he asked them to the individuals as well as to their managers. In addition to finding a strong agreement among employees and their managers about the assessment of the employee's current potential, he found—by following scores of people over decades—that there was indeed a *predictable* pattern of maturation of potential. By predictable, I mean just as reliable as the time-tested growth charts one sees in a pediatrician's office.

Jaques found that potential, the capacity to handle complexity, is not static. It matures throughout one's life, peaking only late in adulthood, often after retirement. Biologically, potential matures. In other words, you become innately more capable of dealing with complexity as you age, whether or not you accumulate new knowledge and skills. It is the combination of this innate maturation of potential and acquired skills that qualifies some people for bigger and bigger roles as they get older. (This is especially good news for those of you who are aging Baby Boomers.)

Now we can begin to piece together these scientifically based concepts to design a system for developing employee capabilities. We need to differentiate the development of an employee to become more effective in his current role from the development of the employee in order to qualify for future roles. The first step is to increase effectiveness today. The second step is to prepare to become effective in bigger roles tomorrow.

How Effective Is He?

Who should be accountable for assessing how effective any particular employee is in his role today and for coaching him to enhance his effectiveness? Because managers are accountable for the effectiveness of their subordinates and for continually improving their capabilities, it makes perfect sense to hold the manager accountable for both the assessment and for the coaching.

Now, what capabilities go into being effective in a role? We have already established that raw intellect is necessary but, by itself, is not sufficient. One also has to have enough role-specific skilled knowledge, to be committed to apply one's capabilities to the work of the role, and to be mature enough to deal with the strains of the role and the working relationships with others.

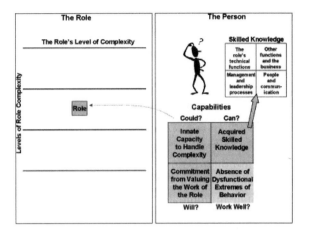

Let's condense these capabilities into four basic questions:

1. Could he/she do the role? This asks whether the employee's raw ability to handle complexity is at the same level as the role's complexity.

2. Can he or she do the role? This asks—given the employee's potential—is he or she knowledgeable and skilled enough to master the actual work of the role.

3. Will he or she do the role? This asks whether the employee values the work of the role sufficiently to fully apply his or her capabilities to succeed in meeting the role's accountabilities.

4. Will he or she work well in the role? This asks whether the employee is mature enough to handle the stresses, uncertainties, tough decisions, and strained working relationships that inevitably occur in demanding work environments.

Another perspective or dimension for comparing an employee's capabilities with the requirements of a role is what I call the Four-by-Four LEAD Matrix,[4] which the graphic above illustrates.

Four-by-Four Lead Matrix

The Four-by-Four LEAD Matrix provides four additional dimensions for looking at skilled knowledge. These additional dimensions include skilled knowledge about:

- The technical functions of the role.
- Other functions in the organization and "the business' at large.
- Management in general and leadership practices in particular.
- People and communications.

Demonstrated-Effectiveness Appraisal

Demonstrated Effectiveness	Effectiveness Appraisal	Types of Results	Degree of Stretch	Degree of Reality
Above/beyond the box	7	Results requiring breakthrough improvements over existing process capabilities	Ulcers	Managing for Fantasy
Outside the box	6 5 4	Results consistent with significant improvements over existing process capabilities / Results consistent with significant optimization of existing process capabilities	Stretch Goals	Aggressively Managing for Reality
Inside the box	3 2 1	Results consistent with existing process capabilities	Usual Goals	Comfortably Managing for Reality

The role's technical and functional knowledge requirements are fairly straightforward and are often similar in roles separated by just one level. But as roles move up the organizational ladder, they interact with more and different kinds of functions, which requires knowledge about those functions.

These higher-level roles also require more information about the products and services, the customers, the competition, and the industry. In addition, all roles operate within many different processes, which also require specific skilled knowledge. One example is that all managers must become skilled in essential leadership practices. Finally, every role requires some level of interaction and communication with other people, although some require far more than others. This, too, demands specific areas of skilled knowledge.

Appraisal of Demonstrated Effectiveness

For a company to just stay even with its competition, it needs to do better each year than the previous one. For a business to pull ahead of the competition, it needs to find ways to continually improve its processes to make them more fundamentally capable. For a company to dominate its industry, it needs to make stunning breakthroughs in process capability. Shouldn't we apply similar criteria when we appraise someone's effectiveness in a role?

Let's call the midpoint in a role's effectiveness requirements fully mastering the role as it has been designed—that is, someone who is fully knowledgeable about the defined processes, has a good work ethic, and is mature, but is not improving on the expected QQT/Rs. Let's call the next quartile of effectiveness consistent with someone who has not only fully mastered the defined role but is adding incremental value (along the four dimensions of relative accountabilities). This value is real, but not permanent—that is, he may have stretched his commitments this year, conserved resources better, and showed better teamworking, but he didn't fundamentally improve the capabilities of the role. The top quartile would be consistent with someone who not only added value this year but found ways to permanently improve the role's capabilities—within his authority limits. To be assessed above the role's maximum required effectiveness would be consistent with all of the above, plus effectively taking on projects that the manager would not otherwise assign to this role or identifying significant innovations yielding breakthrough improvements in capabilities. See the following graphic for a visual explanation of this concept.

One can readily see that these appraisals are not objective. They are subjective judgments made by the manager. In order for this process to have a common standard, to have credibility, and to be considered fair, however, one cannot rely on the isolated or capricious judgments of individual managers. Returning once again to the A-B-C accountability chain, the CEO should first assess all of her immediate subordinate executives against the same standard and be present with them as a group to "gear" their judgments of their subordinates. In this way, the CEO both establishes the standard for the entire organization and is able to judge the effectiveness with which her subordinate managers apply the same standard in evaluating their subordinates. Similarly, the process cascades down and across the entire company.[5]

Go Get 'Em, Coach

The next piece of the puzzle of developing individuals' capabilities is the leadership practice of coaching, the accountability by the immediate manager for enhancing subordinate effectiveness in current role. This begins with the demonstrated effectiveness appraisal (DEA),[6] because in rendering that judgment, managers must first conjure up a mental picture of what the role would look like if it were filled in each of the incremental steps described previsouly. The manager then compares a particular subordinate against that image to see which step of demonstrated effectiveness most aptly describes him. In this way, the manager begins to take inventory—along the lines of the relative accountabilities—of the aggregate value that the subordinate added (or didn't add) during the past year.

Next, the manager considers whether the employee appears to be already working at his full potential. If so, by definition, the employee is fully knowledgeable, committed, and mature. There is no more room for improvement in this role at this time. The coaching would then consist of positive recognition and a discussion of ways to ensure the role remains interesting for the subordinate. But if the manager judges that the employee has the potential to be more effective in this role, he must articulate what the employee was not doing (or was doing wrong) that he could, in fact, be doing better or correctly. This "effectiveness gap" analysis, then, is the starting point for giving managerial feedback (to explain the basis for the DEA) and for explaining the opportunities for development. The next step is to gain agreement with the subordinate about the DEA and any effectiveness gaps. What kinds of skilled knowledge need to be developed? What areas does the subordinate need to focus on better? Which extreme behaviors need to be mitigated or completely overcome?

The final step in this initial phase is to identify those developmental resources. A systematic process of bringing managers together with their common manager to jointly discuss the potential of all employees one and two levels down must be in place. The evaluating manager-once-removed, and a few other managers, must have had at least three months of working contact with each employee being assessed. Under these conditions, the preliminary judgments of current potential are reasonably accurate.

To further improve on the soundness of these judgments, it is essential to delve next into an assessment of employee career (future) potential. The discourse goes something like this: "Let's think about the level she could potentially handle in the future. If she were given all of the developmental support necessary throughout her career and if she were strongly motivated to work at her full potential, then I believe she could function at high Level 6 by career end. This would be yet another level or more over what I think her current potential is." Mind you, one is not rendering a judgment about how likely it is that the individual will be given that opportunity. Rather, one is proffering a judgment that the individual in question is likely to be that bright, and as a result could handle the kind of complexity found at that particular level.

When senior teams work together to discuss, explain, and reconcile their impressions of the current and future potential of employees one and two levels down, they significantly enhance their understanding of those people and the kinds of development they would need to work at or closer to their potential. All of this may sound complicated when you read each step, but like any set of directions they make a whole lot more sense once you actually carry them out. A funny thing managers tell me is that once they learn to think about people in this way, they can never go back to their old ways. As one client recently remarked to me following a talent pool–development project, "It just seems so clear. Now that I have gotten accustomed to thinking this way, nothing else makes sense!"

A Mentor's Perspective

The distinction between coaching and mentoring is clear. The immediate manager should be accountable for appraising subordinate effectiveness and helping her to improve her level of effectiveness in her current role. A mentor, who should be the employee's boss's boss, is accountable for appraising employee current and future potential and helping her explore career avenues consistent with:

1. Her maturing potential.
2. Her interests and aspirations.
3. The likely roles needed to be filled in the future, as predicted from the company's long-term business strategy.

Once the mentor and employee agree on the developmental plans (training, education, special projects, developmental assignments, and so forth), they work together with a frequency and intensity appropriate to the desired rate of career advancement.

The mentoring role, with its presumably broader perspective, should focus on what could be in the employee's future career and how to make that happen. The coaching role should focus on what could help the employee be more effective in her current role and how to make that happen. In general, we talk with our mentors about our careers in the company, not our current work role per se. Such dialogue helps us understand and plan how we can optimally fit into the company's projected big picture.

Seeing What Develops

Now you've seen that understanding, assessing, and developing the potential of employees will be vital to the success of any organization. And you can understand that the rate at which people develop, as well as the ways in which they develop, may vary greatly. You've also seen that coaching and mentoring can be invaluable developmental tools. In Part III, I'll discuss in more detail the

---

[1]The concept of potential was developed by Jaques and Cason in their research described in *Human Capability.*

[2]The distinction between effectiveness appraisal ad and performance appraisal was described by Jaques in *Requisite Organization,* pp. 107–8.

[3]See Jaques, *Progression Handbook.*

[4]Based on Jaques's concept of applied capability in *Requisite Organization.*

[5]Jaques's developments of the concept of the use of judgment by a manager in evaluating and the setting of standards by the manager-once-removed is described in *Requisite Organization,* op. cit.

[6]Jaques first set out the connection between personal-effectiveness appraisal and coaching and merit review in *Glacier Project Papers.*

ways that leaders should relate to their subordinates when they take on the role of coach or mentor in helping them develop their potential.

But first turn to Chapter 7 and explore how to pull all of this potential together by searching for accountability in teams.

Part III:
Platforms of Accountability

In Part II, you learned how to leverage the manager-subordinate relationship to the best advantage of a company and its people. That manager-subordinate relationship is the fundamental building block upon which the company succeeds or fails in achieving its goals on both a day-to-day and a long-term basis. It therefore represents the foundation of an effective, efficient, and accountable organization. But it's only the foundation.

Part III builds upon that foundation to show how we can create accountability among the teams, processes, and leadership systems. These are the platforms, if you will, upon which managers and subordinates operate. Thus, managers must ensure that such platforms are properly structured and led.

The explanations in this section will be more complex than explanations in Part II, because accountability leadership requires ridding an organization of all non-value-adding ambiguity. True accountability leadership calls for precise delineation of accountabilities—not only the fixed and relative ones discussed in Parts I and II, but also direct and indirect accountabilities.

Managers need to take the time to thoroughly think through whether authorities and accountabilities are aligned with their intentions and then accurately defined and understood by their subordinates. So take your time with this section, be patient, and remember that the devil is in the details. My goal in this section is to enable you and other leaders to free your people up to perform the work required to deliver on strategy—and waste no more time on working the system!

Chapter 7
Teams: The Search for Accountability

A couple of years ago, Don Peterson, a senior manager at a major utility, called on The Levinson Institute to help his distribution business unit with problems in its recently implemented cross-functional "key lead teams." Over the previous six months, his manager, Bill Mitchell, the head of the business unit, had been under considerable corporate pressure to streamline processes, reduce headcount, and decrease operating and maintenance expenses. Bill concluded that five areas needed to be examined: costs, employee development, safety, reliability, and new business development.[1]

Bill established five key lead teams with 50 high-potential managers from each of his six line operating units and from all of his subordinate staff functions. He also established five sponsor and five cosponsor roles to be filled by his 10 immediate director-level subordinates. Each team was encouraged to appoint its own team leader and to establish its own agenda. As opportunities or problems surfaced anywhere within the business unit, the appropriate key lead team was to be identified and the issue sent to that team for a solution.

Bill told the teams they were accountable for:

1. collecting, studying, and analyzing data and
2. designing, deciding, and implementing changes in processes, standards, and policies.

They were told, in effect, that they were accountable for improvements in their respective areas—costs, employee development, safety, reliability, and new business development—across the entire business unit.

During our initial data-gathering phase, team members and team leaders identified several issues that consistently interfered with their effectiveness. In this chapter, we will examine the kinds of issues that interfere with effective teamwork and different kinds of teams and, at the end of the chapter, we'll revisit Bill and see how he was able to resolve them in his business unit.

Teeming with Teams

Self-directed teams became something of a business fad in the late 1980s and early 1990s largely due to the popularity of empowerment. Teams and their related cultures and buzzwords were hallmarks of the supposedly more collegial, less-hierarchical environments that many companies sought to foster among spirited individuals working together as equals toward one common goal.

Teams experienced a second surge of popularity in the mid-1990s as the vehicle of choice for process reengineering. Michael Hammer, James Champy, and most of the process-consulting industry that followed recommended getting managers out of the way. Instead, they suggested putting quality-circle-type teams in charge of diagnosing process problems and then solving and implementing process improvements. Hierarchy, they announced, was inherently bad and would always undermine effective processes. Hammer and Champy equated hierarchy with bureaucracy and its self-serving chimneys of functional parochialism. "Teams should be accountable for not only the improvements," they declared, "but for the ongoing process itself."

Not surprisingly, both self-directed work teams and process teams have since gone the way of so many other management fads: They have faded into oblivion, but not before wasting countless hours of overworked, highly responsible, and dedicated employees and leaving them disenfranchised and cynical. As one company's employees were fond of saying, "Be careful when the CEO declares, 'Poof, you're empowered.' Because you haven't been empowered...you've been poofed!"

Debunking the Team-Accountability Myth

Does all that I am saying here mean that teams are "bad," that they are incompatible with accountability leadership? Not at all. But I am suggesting that many of the assumptions about team-related practices are wrong, inherently self-defeating, and destructive to an organization's psychological contracts with its employees.[2] In fact, the most damaging myth is that "team accountability" exists at all and offers the key to the establishment of high-performing teams.

Why do I say this? What's wrong with an organization holding teams collectively accountable for their outputs? After all, "teamworking" requires everyone to pitch in, look out for each other, make adjustments for the betterment of the whole. So why not just hold the entire group accountable? Wouldn't that be a sufficient procedure?

The first question is *who* should hold the entire team accountable? Does the team have a manager, for example? If so, is that manager also accountable for the work of each subordinate on the team?

Or is it one or the other? Is the team manager accountable for the individuals but the team collectively accountable for itself? And if the team is self-directed and doesn't have a manager, what entity would hold the team accountable? A higher-level team? A senior higher-level team? The buck must stop at some point, but *where*?

The fact is that I don't think I'd feel very secure as a shareholder if I could only hold teams accountable for other teams because under this arrangement no one role would be accountable for any lateral work flows.

A second question arises: What happens when most members of the team are highly effective team workers but when one or two others are not, resulting in a net result that the overall team output is weak? Does it make any sense to hold the whole team accountable under these circumstances? Would it be fair to penalize those who demonstrated highly effective teamworking just because their team's overall performance was lackluster?

The third question that comes up is this: *How* would one hold the team accountable? If you pay everyone on the team the same, on what basis do you do so: outputs, cooperation, blind loyalty? Throughout this book, you'll notice that I have identified and referenced the trap of compensating employees on the basis of outputs alone. This mistake would be further compounded if contributions to the team's overall outputs varied considerably among the various team members. Can you fire a whole team? That certainly doesn't seem fair. Yet the myth of "team accountability" has become so institutionalized in so many companies that their employees almost take it for granted.

What, then, is the way out of this vicious circle? Actually, it's a simple repair job, especially if you go back to our basic concepts of fixed and relative accountabilities. You'll recall that a key relative accountability is effectively adjusting one's own plans continually in relation to teammates and cross-functional peers, so as to achieve maximum overall benefit for the organization. This means that each team member should be held *individually accountable* for the effectiveness of his or her own teamworking.

Who, then, must be held accountable for the entire team's effectiveness? The manager of the team, of course! It is his job to ensure that the team's work gets done successfully.

How can the team manager accomplish this? By following five specific guidelines, accountable managers can ensure effective outcomes. These guidelines are:

1. Making certain each subordinate effectively meets his or her own QQT/Rs.
2. Conducting ongoing teamworking meetings.

3. Setting effective teamworking context via two-way discussions with the entire team.

4. Translating that context into clear decision-making frameworks.

5. Holding each subordinate individually accountable for effective teamworking.

A Matrix of Cross-Functional Problems

Cascading hierarchies of manager-subordinate teams are the *accountability backbone* of leadership systems. This implies that all cross-functional process flows are always tied together at some point up the hierarchy pyramid by a manager-subordinate team. Thus one manager, who is accountable for all subordinate functions and for the entire process flow, leads the cross-functional process. I label this accountable manager the process's "crossover-point manager."

Do the accountabilities for teams differ in cross-functional teams? Does the team leader of an ad hoc improvement task force have the same kind of managerial authorities and accountabilities over the attached cross-functional team members as a core-team leader has over his permanent subordinates? And who is accountable for an employee assigned temporarily to an improvement team? His core-team manager? The improvement-team manager? Someone else?

If you answer that he has two managers accountable for his outputs, then no one is genuinely accountable. This, in effect, breaks the accountability chain.

Additionally, do leaders of study-recommendation-improvement teams have different accountabilities and authorities than implementation-coordination-improvement team leaders? Accountabilities for both of these teams are typically dealt with by invoking matrix-manager relationships. Routinely, team members are said to have both straight-line managers (usually, their line manager) and dotted-line managers (typically, the improvement team leader).

We have to do better than these muddled reporting relationships to maintain the clear and internal consistency required for accountability leadership.

The Big Three

Without further ado, the "Big Three" (illustrated on the next page) come to our rescue! Here are three basic types of teams, consistent with accountability leadership:

1. **The core team** is the heart and soul of managerial systems. These permanent, cascading manager-subordinate teams offer the primary means for the accountable, ongoing delegation and integration of work down and across the entire leadership system.

Types of Teams: The Big Three

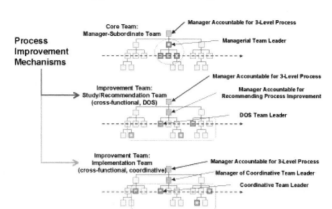

2. **The study-recommendation-improvement team** is the principal means by which managers who "own" cross-functional processes can delegate the accountability down one or two levels to explore opportunities to improve them. By process owner, I mean the first manager up the pyramid who has full managerial authority over all the roles that make up the cross-functional process—again, the crossover-point manager.

All managers are accountable for continually improving the capability (effectiveness), efficiency (low cost), and/or accountability (control) of all resources delegated to them. This is central to the notion of managerial stewardship, the enhancing and taking proper care of resources while using these resources to deliver on QQT/Rs.

But a dilemma occurs the moment a manager accountable for a process attempts to delegate to one subordinate the authority to make decisions and implement changes in that manager's process. The problem is obvious: If one employee decides to change a process that will affect the ability of his teammate or cross-functional peer to meet her accountabilities, we have undermined that second employee's manager's ability to hold her accountable. Once again, we have confounded the accountability chain.

Thus, the process-accountable manager (Manager A), instead, needs to be able to delegate to one subordinate manager (Manager B) the authority to convene a cross-functional team and to appoint a team leader (Team Leader C) to assist Manager B in recommending changes to the accountable Manager A. Manager B then needs to be able to delegate to Team Leader C, the study-team leader, the authority to assign study and design-recommendation tasks to the attached study team members. Team Leader C becomes accountable for recommending improvements to his manager, who, after review, must decide what to recommend to the process-accountable Manager A. Only Manager A, the manager accountable for the process, can decide on these changes after reviewing the implications of the recommendation for meeting his overall accountabilities.

The next dilemma frequently occurs when process-accountable managers want to hold one subordinate accountable for implementing a complex set of process or infrastructure changes across many functional lines. In many companies, this project-manager role is called a process champion or a process owner. This unlucky project manager is frequently given a vague mandate to "get it done" in time and within budget. And then the fireworks begin!

3. **The implementation-coordination improvement team** is the mechanism for avoiding this kind of short circuit. It allows a process-accountable manager to ensure the effective implementation of these improvements down and across his organizational units, without creating another tangled web of matrix relationships with subordinates who have more than one manager.

Again, the principle here is quite straightforward. The way any Manager A accountably implements changes in subordinate processes is to delegate to each individual subordinate Manager $B_{1, 2, 3, \text{etc.,}}$ the QQT/R of implementing her piece of it. If this needs to go down one or two more levels, Manager A once again relies on the cascading A-B-C accountability chain.

However, complex process implementation frequently requires careful orchestration *across* functional lines to ensure the proper synchronization (timing) and articulation (joining) of each functional sub-process into a new, seamless cross-functional process. This is the reasoning behind why project leaders are often mistakenly "given" accountability to implement the changes.

The process-accountable manager (Manager A) cannot delegate the full authority over this total implementation to one individual, but she can delegate to one subordinate manager (Manager B_1) the accountability for "taking the lead" in its coordination. Manager B_1 is then given the authority to establish an ad hoc implementation-coordination team, appointing a Team Leader C_1 (one level down) to have implementation-coordination authority and accountability in relation to her other identified cross-functional peers.

Implementation-coordination authority is more limited than core-team managerial authority and even study-team-leader authority. It requires access to information about the other functions, and the authority to convene and persuade others to find a solution in common. This solution must optimally meet the process-accountable manager's (Manager A's) overall intentions and, simultaneously, meet each of the team members' individual accountabilities.

Failing to coordinate such an integrative solution will require Team Leader C_1 to decide whether to "let it pass" or to "kick it up" to his manager, Manager B_1. Then, Manager B_1 must apply teamworking authority with her colleagues (Managers $B_{2, 3, etc.}$) to find a solution that best supports their core manager's (Manager A's) needs.

Following the thread of accountability, above, may seem difficult at first, but consider the cost of not being clear with process-improvement teams. Enormous amounts of wasted time, energy, credibility, trust, and commitment have been squandered over the past 25 years with ill-defined improvement teams empowered to go off on their own, feeling responsible and believing they were accountable for making process changes. This takes us back to my original thesis that much of an organization's unrealized potential traces back to the lack of accountability leadership.

Three-Level Information Exchange

Another common problem with teams occurs when managers conduct so-called "teamworking" meetings with two or more levels of employees—namely with their core team and one or more additional levels down. This occurs frequently when structures with too many levels and/or poor functional alignment force a manager to go down two or more levels to get key cross-functional roles together in order to make a business decision.

Here is an example from the annals of consultation: A rather large client company, a roll-up IT services company with $5 billion of revenue and 40,000 employees, structured its business-unit-president positions at high Level 5 (see Chapter 4), with COO positions at mid-Level 5 and regional "president" positions at low Level 5. Whenever the business-unit head wanted to meet with all of the Level-4 business functions (marketing, development, services, and sales) to discuss and adjust strategy, he had to meet with two levels of management in between.

Three- or four-level teamworking meetings can cause all sorts of conflicts, the most important of which is that they short-circuit the intervening managers' authorities over their subordinates, making it more difficult to hold them accountable for their subordinates' outputs. When a manager-once-removed

Direction of Output

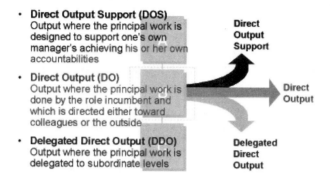

- **Direct Output Support (DOS)**
  Output where the principal work is
  designed to support one's own
  manager's achieving his or her own
  accountabilities

  Direct
  Output
  Support

- **Direct Output (DO)**
  Output where the principal work is
  done by the role incumbent and
  which is directed either toward
  colleagues or the outside

  Direct
  Output

- **Delegated Direct Output (DDO)**
  Output where the principal work is
  delegated to subordinate levels

  Delegated
  Direct
  Output

(Manager A) actively engages her subordinates-once-removed (Subordinates C) in decision-making discussions, she may assign QQT/Rs to them, which are in conflict with existing ones assigned by their own managers (Managers B). Additionally, the Manager Bs may get blindsided by discussions between their own manager (Manager A) and their subordinates (Subordinates C).

This is not to imply that three-level meetings are never appropriate. On the contrary, these meetings are quite useful for information exchange and alignment purposes. Once a major new initiative or process or product change has been agreed upon, it is often valuable to begin its launch with a big-tent meeting. Our prototypical Manager A must make sure that everyone hears the same message from the same individual at the same time, to ask questions and to commit collectively to its success. The key is to ensure that these meetings do not deteriorate into decision-making meetings or complaining sessions.

What Direction Is Your Output?

One of the key requirements of accountability leadership is to avoid internal inconsistencies, such as holding more than one manager accountable for the same employee or two employees accountable for the same output. We have seen how so-called "team accountability" and "self-directed" process-improvement teams can create such disconnects. In order to bring additional clarity to the process of delegation, Elliott Jaques found it useful to differentiate between three kinds of outputs, which are represented in the preceding graphic: those that are directed upward, those that are directed outward, and those that are delegated further downward.

- **Direct-Output Support (DOS).** Output where the principal work goes toward supporting one's own manager in achieving his direct output accountabilities is called direct-output support (DOS). Typical roles delivering largely DOS are financial analysts, executive speechwriters, and secretarial roles.

Because these employees' outputs are usually incorporated into their managers' final outputs, they may be established more than one level below the manager without creating disconnects—the manager, after all, has to decide whether to use their subordinates' outputs. DOS is the only type of QQT/R that a study-recommendation team leader can delegate to an employee temporarily assigned to his team, without undermining that employee's accountable manager. This is because the team leader decides how to use the employee's output (an analysis or recommendation), so the "true" manager is off the hook for that output.

- **Direct Output (DO).** Output where the principal work is directly performed by the subordinate receiving the QQT/R and is then directed outward (neither up nor down) either toward colleagues inside the company or to others on the outside is called direct output (DO). Individual contributor roles, for example, produce mainly DO.

  The manager delegating DO QQT/Rs to subordinates is fully accountable for the subordinate's outputs as though he had produced them himself. He cannot go back to his own manager if a subordinate's output blows up and say, "It's not my fault. You see my subordinate over there? He's the real culprit."

  If a cross-functional team leader (such as a project manager or implementation-coordination team leader) had the authority to delegate DO QQT/Rs to attached employees, it would create confusion as to which manager should be held accountable for that employee's output. Is it the straight-line manager? Is it the dotted-line manager? Accountability leadership requires unambiguous managerial authority and accountability for subordinate outputs.

- **Delegated Direct Output (DDO).** Output where the employee's work gets done by delegating chunks of it down to the next subordinate level (that is, where the employee must also be a manager) is called delegated direct output (DDO). Put another way, any manager who delegates QQT/Rs (to subordinates) as *direct outputs* is generating DDO.

  Only managers of core teams can delegate parts of their accountabilities to subordinates. These managers remain accountable for everything that gets done—or doesn't get done—below them.

Out of the Matrix Maze

With these three types of teams and three directions of output under our belts, we can now get a lot closer to finally eliminating the need to manage cross-functional improvement teams with non-accountable multiple-boss structures or relationships.

Only accountable core team managers can properly delegate all three types of outputs (QQT/Rs) to their subordinates. Study-recommendation team leaders can delegate only DOS outputs to their attached team members. Implementation-coordination team leaders cannot delegate any outputs to other members of their team; they can only convene and attempt to persuade others to make adjustments that will align all of their outputs.

To do otherwise—to authorize a cross-functional team leader to delegate DO or DDO assignments to team members—will always create a disconnect. It will put the team members in potential conflict between doing what their "real" manager is telling them to do ("Don't give away an inch of my function's authority") and what their team leader is pressuring them to do ("Show some courage and be a team player").

This conflict is the source of natural organizational resistance that has spawned a multi-billion dollar consulting and training industry focused on building team passion and empowerment to overcome organizational barriers to team creativity. These negotiation-, interpersonal-, and social-based approaches to affecting cross-functional process improvements represent nothing more than a series of compensatory mechanisms. If we cannot align accountability with authority, we will instead get responsible people to collude with each other to ignore the accountability hierarchy and bull and jam a solution through the system. Although it may work in any given situation, it will always incur the cost of further erosion of accountability, enormous wasted effort, sub-optimization of the whole, and long-term squandering of the good will and commitment of highly responsible employees. It represents the worst of managerial leadership abdication.

An Inventory of Team Pitfalls

Speaking of managerial abdication, one can pinpoint why teams encounter different kinds of problems by knowing exactly what organizational conditions will set problems in motion. I have found three primary categories of such anti-team organizational conditions:

- Inadequate organizational structure
- Inadequate managerial processes.
- Inadequate communication processes.

As you read through these explanations, do you recognize any inadequacies from your own company?

Inadequate Organizational Structure

Five points comprise this inadequacy. The first is too many managerial layers, causing an organization to bloat into a deadly state of bureaucracy. The second, the flip side, involves too few managerial layers, leaving a managerial vacuum.

The other three elements of this category are:

- Poor functional alignment with too high a crossover point, causing an organization that is said to be composed of "functional chimneys."
- Processes structured without clearly accountable managers, meaning that there is no true "process owner."
- Accountabilities of roles and functions not matched by authorities. In such organizations you hear the following phrase quite often: "Sorry, I can't help. My hands are tied."

Inadequate Managerial Processes

I have identified at least nine of these. They run the gamut from failure to set context, an accountability leadership basic, to poor selection processes resulting in the Peter Principle. Here they are in full:

- Failure to set context, or "flying blind."
- Employees held accountable for their own outputs. No excuses allowed.
- Too much competition for the same resources or too few resources available. This is the proverbial setup for failure or, alternatively, an "invitation to conflict."
- Work routinely gets assigned at levels too low.
- Incentives that are output-based. I call this the "carrot-and-stick" approach. This usually invites individuals to maximize their own paycheck at the expense of the team's effectiveness.
- No established cross-functional working relationships, causing a culture of "survival of the fittest."
- Failure to distinguish between core teams and improvement teams, a form of managerial abdication.
- Doing business in three-level information-exchange teams, essentially a managerial "bypass."
- Flawed selection processes—that is, people being over-promoted or promoted for political reasons. Here is where the Peter Principle shows up, again and again.

Inadequate Communication Processes

Obviously, good communication lies at the heart of any successful system. Therefore, I have made communication a category all its own. Here's what it looks like when communication processes are insufficient:

- Employees are not held accountable for effective collegial and cross-functional integrative problem-solving. I call this "sanctioned blinders."

- Employers are not held accountable for communicating and interacting with their employees within reasonably courteous limits.

- Destructive communication runs the show. The organization culture is fraught with blaming.

- Saying one thing while thinking another. This is in contrast with effective communication processes that embraces true problem solving and attempts to pinpoint real obstacles. Instead, everyone is just going through the motions.

Utility Bill Finds Accountability

Remember Bill Mitchell, the business-unit head of the utility company? After reading the team pitfalls in the previous section, you can now imagine some of the difficulties he unwittingly caused by establishing key lead teams to improve unit-wide processes and systems.

To begin, Bill created self-directed work teams. Each team was made up of 10 middle-level managers who were told to elect their own leader. Bill told the teams to decide their own agenda, to design process improvements, and to then decide on and implement them. Bill attempted to provide some guidance for them by establishing sponsors (his own immediate subordinates), but he left the teams with loads of accountability and no true authority. This was the perfect setup for stress and managing for fantasy!

The team members were initially quite excited about being chosen, about being in the limelight, and about having the chance to make a difference. Much to their surprise, they quickly discovered that Bill's immediate subordinates in staff functions (HR, finance, safety, reliability) resented the teams for usurping much of what they perceived to be their own accountabilities. After all, Bill's subordinates felt that they were accountable for "stewarding" these very processes. Furthermore, Bill's line subordinates put very strong pressure on their subordinates, who were attached to the key lead teams, to support only a very narrow range of changes—and mainly ones that would increase *their own* scope of authority.

The team leaders were really in a bind. Because they were so visible, they were vulnerable for suffering the consequences of poor process-reengineering efforts. In particular, they were dumbfounded as to how they could force their own managers (and other director-level managers) to accept changes that the lower-level team came up with.

After two days of accountability leadership consultation, Bill and his team were able to understand the fantasy of expecting significant improvements using the key-lead-team vehicle. It was painful, but Bill moved quickly to rectify his error. Bill immediately set about delegating to his staff directors the accountability for identifying opportunities to improve processes involving their functions. First, they were to do simple feasibility studies. Then, they would establish study-recommendation and implementation-coordination teams to support those improvements that he decided had the greatest payback.

Bill made it clear that he was accountable for setting the context for each phase of each improvement effort. He alone had the authority to decide which recommendations would be implemented, and he would delegate to each of his own subordinates the accountability for implementing their part of these changes.

Even more importantly, Bill and his team began to understand the importance of accountability leadership. They started to systematically align structure and process with strategy and people with roles, and they began to engage the whole business unit with Accountability Leadership practices. Within nine months, Bill's business began to realize gains in productivity on the order of 50-to-60 percent with a reduction in headcount. An added bonus was a significant improvement in morale throughout his entire business unit. Bill's search was over; he had found accountability.

The moral here is that leadership is so much more than pep rallies with hollow exhortations and slogans of empowerment. Accountability leadership requires a clear head, solid principles, and the hard work of systematically applying these principles. It requires a fervent belief that people will only realize their full potential in an employment organization when the system manages for reality, aligning authorities with accountabilities.

As you have seen in this chapter, LEAD applied to teams can yield enormous leverage. As you'll see in the next chapter, when applied to ongoing cross-functional processes, this leverage can be even greater!

---

[1]The concept of new business development as a mainstream function at corporate levels was introduced by Jaques in *Requisite Organization,* p. 44.
[2]Much of the material in this chapter on teams and on DOS, DO, and ADO has been developed from concepts in Jaques, *Requisite Organization,* Part 3, Section 6.

Chapter 8
Making Processes Work: Accountability, Capability, and Efficiency

How productively do you spend your time at work? How much of your time do you spend chasing after people (and the things they're supposed to be doing) in other parts of the company? Does all this prevent you from focusing your time on doing your "real" work?

I regularly hear that far less than half of people's time is spent doing what they are literally paid to do and what they are accountable for. And anywhere from 50-to-80 percent of their time is spent compensating for disconnects elsewhere in the company. Why is this so predictable in so many different industries and in so many different parts of the world?

By now, you must know my answer: a failure to implement accountability leadership! I find that most organizations have a sweep-it-under-the-rug approach to what processes are and how their managers need to integrate, control, and improve them. They have adopted all kinds of quick-fix approaches to shore up these processes, ranging from appointing process owners or champions to teaching everyone negotiation tactics to tying everyone's compensation to outputs from the entire process.

Unfortunately, some very good methods, such as Six Sigma (statistical-process control), have been misapplied to more fundamental aspects of process problems. As you will see in this chapter, the actual roots of many of these problems are in a basic breakdown of the managerial system and not in technical causes at all.

From what you encounter each day at work, you should be able to come up with dozens of war stories of costly cross-functional disconnects. Here is one typical story from the annals of consultation.

A large national service company, doing business in 150 major U.S. branches, negotiated a lucrative truck- and van-purchasing contract with one of the Big

Three automobile manufacturers early in the year 2000. If the branch-purchasing agents throughout the company collectively purchased 500 vehicles from the manufacturer in the fiscal year (at a favorable rate for each unit purchase), the service company would receive an additional $750,000 rebate.

On December 12, 2000, the corporate purchasing VP sent out an e-mail reminding the branch agents that the company was up to 487 vehicles, so they should "push forward purchases to *this* year" to achieve the minimum 500 required.

On January 15, 2001, the data rolled in: 20 additional vehicles had been purchased, but only five of them were from the manufacturer offering the rebate! As a result, $750,000 was down the drain.

Who was accountable for this wasted opportunity? The district purchasing agents were subordinate to operational managers in the branches, not to the corporate purchasing VP. Because of the lack of clear line accountability for purchasing, no one could be held accountable except the CEO—and he is too removed from these kinds of processes to have any direct impact. How can we understand and apply accountability to processes to avoid these kinds of breakdowns?

For most of this book, we have looked at accountability primarily from the perspective of manager-subordinate role relationships that replicate themselves in *vertical* flows through A-B-C accountability linked chains. Manager A holds subordinate Manager B accountable for the outputs of B's Subordinate C and for C's effectiveness in role. In Chapter 7 we began to look at a manager's accountability for the outputs and effectiveness of his entire team. In fact, one can view teamworking itself as a process flow, but one that is *lateral* (or horizontal) rather than vertical in direction.

Thus, every manager of a team is accountable for the effectiveness of the lateral workflow of his or her subordinate teammates.

In fact, every process (including complex cross-functional processes) can be viewed as workflows across a pyramid of manager-subordinate core teams, cascading down and across that organizational unit. And the manager at the top of the pyramid is the process-accountable manager. (See the illustration on the next page.)

In this chapter, we will examine many aspects of processes and introduce another dimension to accountability: direct and indirect accountabilities. We will explain why so many organizations resort to matrix-reporting relationships (that is, straight- and-dotted-line managers) in a self-defeating attempt to improve the effectiveness of their process flows. And we will introduce a systematic approach to building accountable cross-functional processes.[1]

Accountability, Capability, and Efficiency

We have already explored how process-accountable managers, sitting on top of cross-functional process pyramids, can deliver on their accountability for

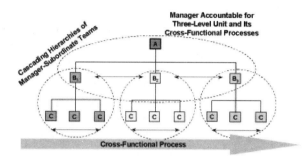

the continual improvement of their processes. They cannot delegate wholly the accountability for improving their cross-functional process to any one subordinate, because that will interfere with the manager's ability to hold his other subordinates (who also use part of that process to meet their objectives) accountable.

The solution to this apparent dilemma called for the use of two types of cross-functional improvement teams: study-recommendation teams and implementation-coordination teams. These teams assist the process-accountable manager in making and implementing process-change decisions. Can these concepts also help us out now in our attempt to explain how the process-accountable manager can ensure that each of his processes are optimally and simultaneously accountable, capable, and efficient, on an *ongoing* basis?

First, let's get clear about some definitions:

- An *accountable* process is one that is in control. It delivers the goods not only capably and economically, but also consistently and reliably—within all limits that have been defined.

- A *capable* process is one that can do what it was established to do. It can deliver the function, create the outputs, and provide the throughput intended.

- An *efficient* process is one that can do its work economically. It requires a minimal amount of expense, consumables, and time.

My contention is simple: Any process-accountable manager who fails to deliver processes satisfying all three of these conditions simultaneously is failing to meet his process-stewardship accountabilities.

As you saw in Chapter 7, capability, in core (manager-subordinate) teams, is achieved accountably through sound managerial and teamworking leadership by:

1. Establishing the right roles and defining their accountabilities clearly.
2. Filling the roles with capable people and developing their effectiveness in role.
3. Setting clear, two-way context, both upward (big picture) and downward (teamworking), and translating it into decision-making frameworks.
4. Defining ambitious, yet achievable, QQT/Rs.
5. Ensuring that each subordinate team member delivers on his or her fixed and relative accountabilities—especially effective teamworking—within the decision-making frameworks.

This becomes the starting point for understanding how to achieve capability in cross-functional processes. Every process-accountable Manager A must exercise effective managerial and teamworking leadership with his subordinate Managers B and then ensure that they do the same with their subordinates. Accomplishing this is half the battle, because Subordinates C will then be effectively engaged with their own teammates (within subordinate Manager B's framework) and within Manager A's intentions for the overall cross-functional process.

Additionally, we can expect effective, dynamic adjustments within the process at two levels. The subordinate Manager Bs are accountable for exercising effective teamwork at a process-macro level. Their Subordinate Cs are accountable for exercising teamwork within each function at a process-micro level. Optimal process capability is achieved when managers and subordinates make timely, flexible, and accurate adjustments in their own work approaches in relationship to the requirements of others in order to best support the overall needs of the entire organizational unit.

Stop Cross-Functional Gridlock

In order to deliver optimal capability, we need a means for ensuring similarly dynamic adjustments between employees *across* functional lines. These are people who do not have the same manager. They are people who work in the same process flow, but not on the same team. To address this type of cross-functional working relationship, I need to address the concepts of direct and indirect accountabilities. Take a look at the graphic on the next page for a visual explanation of the process.

Let's look at the kind of breakdown that could be avoided completely if one individual on one team had a predetermined accountability to *initiate* some action toward another individual on another team—an indirect accountability for the process itself.

Cross-Functional Working Relationships

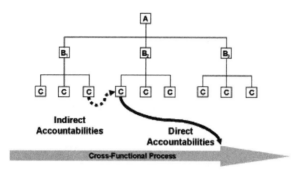

A wire-manufacturing plant has three sequential production areas, going from billets to wire rod to wire, each under the control of an area supervisor and, collectively, under a single manufacturing superintendent. The superintendent also has a maintenance supervisor under him. The plant always runs at full capacity. Time for repairs and maintenance is tight but extremely important to find. A modest amount of inventory is kept between the three areas in order to keep the lines running during the usual number of brief production stoppages.

In spite of this, supervisors in the two down-line units and the maintenance supervisor are constantly frustrated when stoppages up-line last longer than the small inventory. They are not notified immediately about the delays. In many instances, they can squeeze in 30 minutes of maintenance work if given less than 15 minutes notice. Instead, machine operators and mechanics are sitting idle for more than 45 minutes. This means significant cost to the overall plant productivity and delivery performance.

Wouldn't you think that some machine operator upstream would feel *responsible* for alerting someone on the downstream units when a breakdown occurred? Occasionally someone does. But more often than not, everyone up-line is running helter-skelter trying to fix the up-line problem. They don't have time to think about any down-line problem and they figure the delay won't last very long. And besides, they are not even sure they even had the authority to call ahead.

Trivial problem? Absolutely not! The company loses hundreds of thousands of dollars annually in direct costs and even more in opportunity costs. Complicated solution? Well, let's take a look.

What if the superintendent sits down in the following manner with his four supervisors in a regular team meeting?

- The superintendent sets context about this problem and its effect on delivering the overall strategy.
- He then tells each of the production supervisors that they are accountable for alerting the other three when a stoppage is likely to last longer than 15 minutes.
- He can then request that each supervisor identify the machine-operator position on his team that would be accountable for advising the other teams if these conditions arose.
- The supervisors should also clarify which role(s) on their own teams should be alerted by the other team's advisor and how priorities for mobilizing the maintenance crew should be decided.

Giving Good Advice

What have we done here? Each supervisor always has a general teamworking accountability to make adjustments in relation to each other to best support the superintendent's overall objectives. In addition, each supervisor is now specifically accountable for getting information upstream and downstream under certain stoppage conditions. Finally, specific operators, two levels down from the superintendent, are given authority to advise specific individuals on other teams under those same conditions. And these operators are held accountable for doing so effectively.

Each operator now has two kinds of accountabilities. He has a *direct* accountability for running his own machine effectively, within limits, and for producing defined outputs. He also an *indirect* accountability in relation to other operators to advise them about delays. This advice allows the other operators to do their work more effectively.

Advising requires three kinds of authorities:

1. The authority to be kept informed about what is going on in another role's area.
2. The authority to judge what would be useful information to give to the other role under conditions warranting this accountability.
3. The authority to gain access to the individual in the other role in order to share the information.

The individual being informed has full discretion as to how she will act on this information. The effectiveness of that individual will be judged by her immediate manager. That manager can be confident that this subordinate received the proper information upon which his or her decisions and actions are based. This indirect advising accountability, in other words, is a means by which the process-accountable manager (in our example, the superintendent) can ensure that everyone working within his cross-functional process will make optimal adjustments to the process flow in order to maximize its accountability, capability, and efficiency.

As we are about to see, advising is one type of a more general *informing* accountability. Informing accountability does not require the authority to instruct or even persuade another role to use the information. It simply needs the authority to effectively inform them.

Win Friends? Influence People?

The key to getting the optimal cross-functional process is to first decide on the vertical structures (that is, cascading manager-subordinate functional teams) that are best aligned with strategy, on the one hand, and with sound process flows on the other. With strong managerial and teamworking leadership and effective employee development, also make sure each individual with direct accountabilities for the process is working effectively and within the process-accountable manager's context. In particular, each employee must be encouraged to think "outside the box," exercising judgment and discretion to initiate creative solutions to the role's challenges, and still operate "inside the box." Additionally, rely on appropriately defined lateral (indirect-accountability) working relationships to *influence* and/or *regulate* the choices being made by those direct-output employees to ensure maximum adaptability still consistent with process control.

However, let the manager beware! My experience consistently points out that the process will always *degrade* if:

1. Value-adding indirect accountabilities are *not* made explicit.
2. The boundary conditions governing their use are *not* made clear.
3. The process-accountable manager's context has *not* been accurately communicated to subordinates within the process flow.

By the time responsible people finally act to resolve some disconnect or ambiguity, it is often too little and too late. This is a prime example of how accountability leadership seeks to eliminate non-value-adding ambiguities from the system in order to free people to fully exercise their judgment and discretion on matters that add genuine value. Once again, accountability leadership helps free people to do their work—not to work the system!

The table on page 122 expands upon the theme of defining a hierarchy of value-adding indirect accountabilities and authorities, the purpose of which are to support the process-accountable manager in having accountable, capable, and efficient processes.

CATEGORY	ACCOUNTABILITY	AUTHORITY	CONDITION
Informing	Advising	To take the initiative to provide specialized, critical information to specified roles, which they must decide how to use	To make available information that is judged relevant to the unique issues of another role
	Recommending	To make recommendations to others about trade-offs they should consider while making complex decisions	To model alternative choices for another role, but not to persuade about any particular decisions
Persuading	Coordinating	To convene others in order to persuade them to agree on a common direction, and, if unsuccessful, to delay action until decided at a higher level	Needed when a plan or process must be well synchronized and/or strongly integrated
	Monitoring	To persuade others to adjust their actions, when they are judged to be working at the edge of defined limits for the process	Needed to ensure that processes are simultaneously reliable, in control, capable, and adaptive
Instructing	Auditing	To instruct others to stop taking further actions when they are judged to be working outside of defined limits	Necessary to ensure system or process integrity in relation to critical boundary conditions
	Prescribing	To instruct others to take preauthorized emergency actions under extreme conditions	Triggered by extreme exposures or threats to health, safety, and/or the environment

Managers who are accountable for subordinate cross-functional processes and are implementing accountability leadership need to be vigilant. They must be ready to identify those process steps that are vulnerable to becoming:

- Isolated.
- Narrowly focused.
- Unconnected from other process steps.
- Close to the "edge of the envelope."
- Out of control.
- Subject to quickly unfolding emergencies.

These are conditions that threaten to undermine the accountability, capability, and efficiency of a process.

Isolated? Rx: Advising

As we saw in the wire-plant example, production areas downstream were isolated from critical information upstream that would have supported a more flexible mobilization of maintenance (and production) resources under stoppage conditions. In this case, establishing *advising* working relationships was sufficient to completely solve this problem. This type of informing accountability ends once the information has been shared. As I said previously, it then becomes fully within the discretion of the individual being advised as to how to act on that information. His effectiveness in dealing with stoppage conditions will be evaluated by his own manager. But it is critical that the information be available in order for him to arrive at the best decisions.

Other examples of roles that frequently have a strong advising accountability are ones that have external policy-tracking functions (HR, environmental, governmental, and so forth). These roles are usually in the best position to advise other internal roles about changes or developments that they should take into account when formulating and adjusting their own plans.

Narrowly Focused? Rx: Recommending

Another form of informing accountability is the requirement for one role to perform analyses on data, to model alternatives, and to then recommend possible courses of action to another role in another function. Examples of roles with these types of indirect accountabilities are financial analysts, compensation specialists, legal advisors, and OD specialists. This represents an ongoing accountability to be kept informed about activities in certain functions, to understand the thinking of the people operating in those areas, and to anticipate the kinds of trade-offs they should be considering.

A role with recommending accountability needs authorities similar to those of advising. It differs primarily in the greater degree of analysis done on behalf of the role receiving the recommendations. As with advising, it is for the receiving role alone to decide on how—or even whether—to utilize the recommendation.

Unconnected from Other Process Steps? Rx: Coordinating and Monitoring

At a higher level of cross-functional influence than informing is persuading. This accountability exists in two forms: coordinating and monitoring.

Coordinating

The purpose of coordinating is to generate a strong degree of focus, synchronization, and articulation between several roles that are all working on some aspect of the same process.

For example, many large corporations are finding it increasingly important to develop a high-level branding function. Typically, these roles are part of a corporate marketing group but are not directly accountable for the myriad of market analysis and advertising functions in the same corporate group or in other marketing departments existing within the multiple business units around the world. Each business-unit head is typically accountable for developing his own unit's marketing strategies and promotional materials in concert with the corporate branding strategy. But the actual day-to-day marketing-branding interactions often occur two or three levels down in the organization. In order to ensure corporate-wide branding consistency, a role within corporate branding may be given coordinating accountability with respect to the business-unit marketing roles.

Without a clear definition of this indirect accountability, or clear context governing the corporate branding intent, or clear expectations that the business-unit heads will be held accountable for working within the corporate branding strategy, the central market-branding position is thwarted and compromised from the start. The options for achieving a common brand approach—given lots of accountability without any defined authority—range from endlessly communicating about the importance of a common strategy, cajoling, pleading, threatening, and even extorting the marketing folks in the field to adhere to a common message.

The problem is that each market has different cultures, different interests, and different needs. Field people sometimes feel these are not consistent with the branding message foisted upon them. They are under considerable pressure from their own managers to maximize sales in their region; they want to conserve their resources for messages most carefully tailored to their audience. So, for the best of reasons, a central branding role and many field marketing roles may have genuine differences of opinion about which messages, delivered in what ways, will be best for their unique business needs.

This tension, caused by competing, legitimate organizational needs, is real. It should not be ignored by slogans of empowerment or obliterated by the imposition of rigid rules and regulations. It calls for people, well-informed by their immediate manager as to their local context as well as the crossover-point manager's global context, to reason together. They continue to press for alternative solutions, until constructing one that will best integrate all needs. To accomplish this, the branding coordinator must continually evaluate the presence or absence of convergence and internal consistency of each unit's message in relation to the CEO's corporate message.

This indirect accountability requires the authority to gain access to the plans and progress of the field marketing functions and to compare that work with the corporate branding plan. If the coordinator perceives an important disconnect, he requires the authority to:

- Convene the other roles.
- Explain the problem to the field people and the consequences of not resolving it.
- Persuade the field people to construct and agree on a common course of action that will resolve the global problem and still allow each to meet his or her individual accountabilities.

Failing to achieve such a consensus, the coordinator must have the authority to inform his manager (that is, a member of the crossover-point manager's core team) of the problem, so that the manager can attempt to resolve the matter by way of teamworking. Only if the teammates at this B level fail to resolve the problem is it necessary to bring it to the process-accountable Manager A to decide.

The fundamental difference between informing and persuading is straightforward: In informing, the decision about how to use information is wholly up to the receiving employee, the one with direct accountability. In persuading, a higher level of tension is deliberately placed between the cross-functional roles. This requires more active discussion and debate between them in order to construct an optimal solution. The crossover-point manager should consider establishing this type of indirect working relationship in order to keep the resolution of legitimate—but potentially competing—needs of different functions at the lowest appropriate level in the process flow. If context has been effectively set by the process-accountable manager and accurately communicated by his subordinate managers to employees within the process flow, those employees should be able to regularly construct optimal solutions by themselves. There is no need to kick the problem upstairs.

Monitoring

The second form of persuading accountability is monitoring. This indirect accountability tends to move one role from simply influencing another (cross-functional) role's decisions and actions more toward *regulating* them. We've seen how coordinating attempts to get several people to reconcile their local needs against a more global set of integrative requirements. Monitoring is typically between two roles. It attempts to preserve the balance between exercising creative initiative at the edge of a process's limits, on the one hand, and not undermining the integrity of that process on the other.

There are literally hundreds of examples of value-adding monitoring accountabilities in business organizations. These range from obvious quality-assurance monitoring roles to almost any function that is involved in stewarding a process (financial, HR, marketing, manufacturing, engineering, environmental, safety, and so forth). The intention of this type of indirect accountability is less policing other roles than it is trying to help them find alternative actions that will not get too close to "the edge of the envelope" but will still permit creative initiative.

Out of Control? Rx: Auditing

The most-powerful level of indirect accountability is *instructing*. By this I mean that one role has the authority to overrule another in a lateral relationship (that is, not its subordinate) and can, literally, instruct that person to stop doing something or request that he initiate some emergency action. These are *auditing* and *prescribing,* respectively. Clearly, this type of cross-functional regulating accountability should be reserved for the most serious situations. It should only be used when established well-defined limits have already been violated.

Examples of roles requiring auditing accountability and authority are in the areas of safety, health, environment, legal compliance, and quality control in the pharmaceutical industry. Whenever the safety or health of people, the company, the environment, or the customer is at risk by a process, it is critical to establish clear and unequivocal boundaries and to identify which roles have the accountability to ensure that those boundaries are adhered to. Often, it is only the employee's manager who needs to be accountable for overseeing those limits. At other times, formal regulating accountabilities need to be established laterally to ensure more active vigilance at the edges of the process.

Instructing a peer to stop doing something when he is already clearly outside defined limits doesn't interfere with that employee's relationship with his manager. Remember that the manager is already accountable for ensuring that his subordinates operate within limits.

Subject to Quickly Unfolding Emergencies?
Rx: Prescribing

The prescription is prescribing? Curious though this may sound, the term "prescribing," as in prewritten, has its roots in medicine.

Physicians who have life-and-death decisional authority over patients' lives need to prescribe interventions that must be administered by pharmacists or nurses who are not the physicians' immediate subordinates. This is not simple requesting of a service. It is an instruction that must be followed by the other practitioners unless it violates some existing set of policies or procedures.

In situations that could rapidly deteriorate into a disaster, it is critical to define emergency procedures as clearly as possible, well ahead of time, and to identify which roles under what conditions have the limited manager-like authority to instruct others (who are not subordinates) to follow them. This, again, does not undermine managerial accountability for those subordinates, because prescribing authority, similar to auditing authority, is narrowly defined and only triggered under extreme conditions.

Roles requiring prescribing accountability and authority can be found in disaster-response roles for hospitals, dangerous manufacturing situations, and other potentially explosive conditions. In general, any situation where an immediate, orchestrated, pre-planned emergency response is necessary to avoid major harm to life, the environment, or the organization's viability requires prescribing accountability. But keep in mind that prescribing accountabilities should be reserved for only the most serious potential problems.

Influencing and Regulating: Is That All There Is?

Actually, that is *not* all there is. When one looks at the universe of lateral or indirect working relationships that exist naturally within cross-functional processes, two other types emerge: *service-giving* and *support for process improvement.* Once again, we find that most business organizations have no real concept of organizational accountability or of managerial leadership. These companies resort to various matrix, team, or empowerment solutions to very real process needs.

The common trend in the late 1980s and 1990s was the concept of internal customers and suppliers. This questionable phenomenon persists in many companies today. When support functions, which exist largely to serve other mainstream business functions internally, became too inwardly or bureaucratically focused, many organizations reasoned that they are not "customer-oriented" enough. With recent advances in customer-satisfaction research and a stronger emphasis in business on satisfying the customer, it was not a big leap to reposition internal service givers as suppliers and the internal business functions as customers.

This led to a mushrooming industry of training—especially negotiation training—to improve the responsiveness, quality, and general proactive nature of the service-giving silos. Internal functions spend considerable time and effort negotiating costs, pricing, and charge-transfers in order to increase the competitive pressures upon the service functions to improve. "We'll bring a free-market economy inside our company," is the rallying cry. An inspired solution? No. A big problem? Yes.

Pressed into Service

The relationship between a supplier company and its genuine customer is markedly different from the ideal relationship between an internal service giver and an internal service requester. For one thing, the vendor company's goal with respect to a true customer should be to maximize its own value in every transaction and to decide which customers it wants to be doing business with in order to best serve its business objectives. On the other hand, an internal service-giving function is an organizational resource that needs to be optimally deployed across the entire company in order to best support the company's *overall* objectives—not the function's own objectives.

This is another flagrant example of managerial abdication. Executives routinely fail to establish sound, internally consistent, and adequately "resourced" managerial leadership systems. They reason that responsible, creative managers should be able to work out among themselves ways to divvy up the resources they need. And if the service-providing functions are inefficient or ineffective, then, the managers contend, "we'll set up competition to pressure them into shaping up."

Instead of taking the time to define and "resource" the requirements of implementing their strategy, executives push the problem down one, two, or more levels and allow Darwinian forces to sort it out. Instead of holding the managers of each service function accountable for the quantity and quality of the service she delivers, internal customers hold their feet to the fire. What a waste of time and energy! This is clearly an irresponsible way to treat employees.

The answer, again, is to define service-giving (and service-getting) as an indirect accountability. It constitutes a lateral working relationship that is a true accountability. It is an obligation to deliver a service (if the requester is authorized) exactly as specified (quantity and quality), but not necessarily within the time frame requested. A manager has the authority to re-adjust the timing of any of the QQT/Rs she delegated to a subordinate at any time. A service-getter, on the other hand, can only wait in line unless the process-accountable manager has developed a decision-making framework, within which all people who have requested services must agree to adjust their own priorities for the timing of that service. Service-giving is indirect, because the actual input into a process (the direct accountability) is usually by the service getter. The service giver is indirectly supporting the process through someone else.

Making Processes Work

The ultimate accountability for improving any resource resides with the manager who "owns" that resource. In my consultation and in the Levinson seminars, I refer to this indirect accountability as *support for process improvement.* If the resource is a cross-functional process, then the process-accountable manager owns it. We define this ownership role as the first managerial position on the process pyramid that has full managerial authority over all of the roles with direct input into that process.

For many enterprise-wide processes, this accountability can reside only with the corporate CEO, who, as the CEO of the national service company at the beginning of this chapter was, is too far removed from the actual process to know how to go about specifically improving it. Thus, in order to meet his accountability for the continual improvement of subordinate processes, the process-accountable manager must frequently delegate parts of his accountabilities to subordinates to support him in this endeavor.

We have already explored some of the difficulties this creates for the process-accountable manager. He cannot delegate to one subordinate the full authority to change a process when that might prevent other subordinates from meeting their accountabilities. But the process-accountable manager can delegate to any one subordinate:

1. The accountability for gathering information about the process in order to identify and recommend opportunities for improvement.
2. The authority to establish a study-recommendation team to design the potential improvements and recommend them to the process-accountable manager.
3. The accountability for implementing each functional piece of a change (that the process-accountable manager first decides on) to each functional subordinate.
4. The authority to establish an implementation-coordination team to coordinate the synchronization and articulation of each function's effort in relation to the process-accountable manager's overall intentions.

My intention here is to provide a proactive and accountable mechanism for process-accountable managers, those managers at the top of their pyramids, to be able to continually identify, pursue, and effectively implement changes to their cross-functional processes. The specific mechanisms for improving processes are summarized as follows:

1. Improvements can be made to the process *accountability* by refining structure, establishing value-adding direct and indirect working relationships, and reinforcing accountable managerial leadership practices.
2. Improvements can be made to the process *capability* by improving the technical capabilities of a process, establishing more effective decision-making frameworks, enhancing employee effectiveness in their teamworking and indirect relationships, and reinforcing accountable managerial leadership practices.
3. Improvements can be made to the process *efficiency* by removing steps (and roles) found to not add value to the process, enhancing employee effectiveness in resource stewardship and indirect relationships, and by reinforcing accountable managerial leadership practices.

In this chapter, we explored the universe of indirect working relationships used to improve process effectiveness. These eight categories are advising, recommending, coordinating, monitoring, auditing, prescribing, service-giving, and providing support for process improvement.

As you have seen, there is no escaping the need for a clear means for ensuring accountability, capability, and efficiency in lateral processes and working relationships across functional lines. As the story unfolds in Chapter 9, you will explore ways to effectively align leadership systems and enhance employee effectiveness.

---

[1]Many of the ideas in this chapter (e.g., advising, coordinating, auditing, prescribing, and service-giving) have been adapted from Elliott Jaques; original development of the articulation of cross-functional working relationships in *Requisite Organization,* Part 3, Section 6.

Chapter 9

Aligning the Leadership System

A client of mine in a mid-cap chemical-engineering business was having difficulty with two of his key business units—at least, with what the company called business units. These units consisted mainly of sales, marketing, and product marketing functions. All of the R&D, manufacturing, and engineering/technical services that supported the units' business, however, were located within "technical" functions, external to the business unit.

The company had restructured four years earlier in order to improve its customer focus by aligning its sales and marketing organizations to separate industries, instead of to products, as it had done for decades. Customers had been complaining about receiving multiple sales calls from the same company, and the salespeople internally often competed with each other for the same customer dollar. As a result, the CEO decided to develop market-centric business units. Yet, because he wasn't confident that the new business-unit heads could effectively manage the highly technical research, manufacturing, and services functions, he kept them as separate silos remaining subordinate to him.

In order to give the business-unit heads profit-and-loss accountability, he established a matrix of technical functions running horizontally across the vertical phantom "business units." The so-called product directors within each business unit headed up cross-functional teams made up of commercial and technical people on them, to develop business plans for each market. The directors were then given "contracting" authority with the technical functions to invest in research and to commit the portion of their manufacturing and service-provisioning capabilities deemed necessary to meet the business unit's objectives.

To further complicate matters, the CEO decided to also give the heads of the technical functions (who used to run product-service businesses) P&L accountability as well, just, as he proudly proclaimed, "to keep everyone honest!"

Yet, after two to three years, the smaller business units began to fall farther and farther behind meeting their annual marketing and sales targets. These business-unit heads were frustrated that the R&D groups were continually slipping on their commitments. The R&D groups complained that the largest business unit, which generated more than half of the company's profit, was always preempting the deployment of the best R&D resources toward *its* pet projects.

And while the large business was doing quite well in its market, selling and delivering multiple improved products and services, the net profitability of the entire company was going down.

Matters became even worse when the business "product directors" within the smaller units requested R&D to make changes or adjustments in direction because of a change in their business' market. The R&D directors, already frustrated at having several bosses, began to push back by saying that the CEO was really their manager and that he was holding them accountable for objectives incompatible with the business unit requests. R&D directors emphatically responded to the product directors, "Hey, buzz off!"

This somewhat convoluted structure is not unlike what we see in many companies today. Just by telling someone that he has P&L accountability doesn't mean that person has, in reality, sufficient authority to direct, "resource," adjust, integrate, and control the actions of all of the functions, which must work together to create the business result. A conflicted manager might finally blurt out, "If you are going to want me to be accountable for profit and loss, I need the requisite authority to conduct business!"

Strategic Alignment's Second Coming

Cycles of centralization and decentralization occur with such regularity in business that they are generally taken for granted. For several years, centralization will be in vogue with economies of scale, functional specialization and standardization, and central pools of specialists for rapid deployment. During the next few years, problems arise because of it (bureaucratic silos, self-serving processes, inward-looking planning, poor cross-functional working, and loss of business and customer focus). Then decentralization comes back with nimble units, market-responsive business changes, good teamworking, and greater initiative. During the next several years, its problems also come into focus (high overhead, lack of process control, poor synergy across businesses, and business fortresses). It reminds me of the movie *Groundhog Day,* where one is destined to replay the mistakes of the past over and over and over again.

Why do intelligent and otherwise pragmatic businessmen and businesswomen seem so adrift in these raging crosscurrents of business fads, surfing them seemingly at random? As I have been saying throughout this book, the lack of any clear definitions and scientifically validated concepts of managerial leadership systems are the real culprits. In the absence of a true body of knowledge and the

Business-Unit Functions
Alignment of Mainstream, Resourcing, and Stewardship Functions

engineering principles that derive from it, people are doomed to select ad hoc approaches to design their strategy. And they become vulnerable to the simplistic solutions offered up by business gurus and business schools. The business press, eager to report on the next new, sexy theory, tends to reinforce this vulnerability.

Building on the work of Elliott Jaques,[1] it is now possible to accurately translate an organization's business strategy into a range of alternative, feasible structures and to then test each one against my three criteria: accountability, capability, and efficiency.

An architect has many options for designing a building. Should it be, for example, an I-beam or a cantilevered beam? Both options must conform to basic properties of physics and engineering. The architect can arbitrarily choose to defy the laws of gravity, but the results could be disastrous. Similarly, a critical component of strategic leadership is the design of one's organizational system for delivering on that strategy. Here as well it is necessary to adhere to a set of organizational-design principles consistent with accountability leadership. Leaders cannot wisely choose to ignore the laws of aligned accountability-authority and complexity-judgment.

Four Building Blocks of Structure

The term "organizational structure" is often bandied about, but what is organizational structure *really* all about?

An organization's structure is the means for distributing decision-making authority, within a delegation-accountability framework. It is a way of placing one's bets as to the best way to align roles with different levels of complexity, with different functions, and contributing to different process flows. It allows the assignment of categories of authority to various functions in such a way as to ensure the proper deployment of all the accountabilities necessary for doing business.

There are four dimensions of structure. Levels of role complexity were discussed in Chapter 3, and three-level processes were examined in Chapter 8. This chapter addresses the third and fourth dimensions: functional alignment and system stewardship, respectively.

Levels of Role Complexity

The first requirement when designing an organization is to identify the number of levels it needs and to ensure that the distances between manager roles and subordinate roles are optimal. Accurately identifying the levels of complexity enables senior management to structure the "right" number of managerial layers in the organization. The correct distance between these levels must be close enough for managers to add value, yet far enough to allow subordinates enough room to effectively apply judgment.

Three-Level Processes

The second element of structure is the establishment of cross-functional processes in such a way that ensures that roles with important lateral working relationships have their crossover-point manager precisely two levels up. The key to effectively integrating and controlling cross-functional processes is to ensure effective lateral communication among employees working within the same processes. This requires that each of them receives specific and accurate context about how his role is expected to support common objectives. Because context is a three-level (A-B-C) communication, the structure requires that key C-level interactions support the same skip-level Manager A.

Functional Alignment

In this chapter, we will deal with a third element of structural design necessary for developing a strategically aligned organization. There is an underlying architecture to the functional alignment of business units within a larger organization. This pattern flows from a basic understanding of what it means to "do business." Once an organization decides how to best translate its strategy into distinct and competitive markets, it should begin by designing fully accountable business units for each market and then aligning them into portfolios providing synergy among those businesses.

System Stewardship

We will conclude this chapter by presenting a structural model for ensuring system and process integrity down and across the entire organization. A central dilemma created by managerial accountability systems is how to ensure the

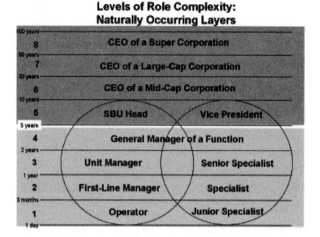

Levels of Role Complexity:
Naturally Occurring Layers

8	CEO of a Super Corporation	
7	CEO of a Large-Cap Corporation	
6	CEO of a Mid-Cap Corporation	
5	SBU Head	Vice President
4	General Manager of a Function	
3	Unit Manager	Senior Specialist
2	First-Line Manager	Specialist
1	Operator	Junior Specialist

consistency and reliability of systems (financial, HR, process control, marketing, and so on) across the entire organization *laterally* and *vertically*, when the accountability chain is only vertical (A-B-C). The key is to think about unit systems as being nested within parent systems of the same type, repeated progressively upwards, until the corporate system, which can only be *owned* by the CEO.

Mind Your Own Business

The functional model that follows reflects a basic underlying architecture of organizational units at all levels. Mainstream or operational-spine managers at every level of an organization are accountable for:

- Doing the work of their function.
- "Resourcing" the work.
- Stewarding the resources.

Whether these managers delegate pieces of these accountabilities to subordinates or whole departments, they remain accountable for all three activities.

The essence of trading effectively in a marketplace is balancing the efforts and resources necessary to effectively:

1. Define marketplace need.
2. Develop improvements in existing products and services.
3. Provide products and services in the most efficient way possible.
4. Sell those products and services to achieve the overall mission of the business as well as its financial objectives.

This defines the mainstream business functions necessary for a business-unit head to be accountable for doing business. They are marketing, development, provisioning, and sales. The business-unit head does not necessarily have to have all these functions directly subordinate to him, but he must have sufficient *authority* to:

1. Direct the activities of each of these functions in relation the unit's overall business plan.
2. Integrate the thinking, decisions, and interactions of the people working in these functions by setting context ("big picture" and teamworking) in regular teamworking meetings.
3. Call people (within the functions) to account for meeting their commitments.

With the starting point that true P&L accountability requires sufficient authority over all four mainstream business functions, we can now address some of the most common organizational myths about business units. To begin, let's revisit the case that I outlined earlier in the chapter.

The chemical-engineering company structured its business units with very few functions truly subordinate to the business-unit (BU) head. In fact, only product-service marketing and sales technical support were genuinely subordinate. There was no customer marketing or advertising, no development, and no provisioning.

The COO was the manager of a central-marketing group as well as of the BU heads. The so-called technical functions (R&D, engineering, tech services, and manufacturing) were all subordinate to the CEO.

The intended relationship between the BUs and all of the other mainstream business functions was a mixture of teamworking, service-giving (and service-getting), and contracting. Because of these ill-defined, lateral accountability relationships, the people working in each of these functions found themselves in a constant state of confusion. They were torn between supporting the competing business-unit requests and their own managers' functional-technical requirements. At the same time, they were caught up in the conflict between the larger BUs and the smaller ones.

Typically, in this kind of multiple-BU, matrix structure, it is the largest BU, or the one generating the most profit or revenue, that gets first dibs on the resource-constrained development and provisioning functions. Here is yet another example of survival of the fittest in large organizations. Calling the smaller BU heads to account for failing to meet their targets is frustrating for everyone. Everyone is locking horns. The COO feels everyone is blaming someone else. The BU heads feel they are set up to fail.

This structural approach, which I maintain, short-circuits the accountability system and breeds political behavior. The senior executives usually got to their high levels by learning how to "work" the system. Their own unit's needs are met at the expense of others. They are quickly identified as the "go to" leaders who know how to make things happen. When they reach more senior levels, they don't have any other model for ensuring that everything below them gets done. They are constantly frustrated by those BU heads who try to play by the rules but always come up short, or they are upset with some BU heads who do get results but are resented by their peers for cornering the shared resources and ultimately suboptimizing the overall business.

The principle here is simple: large organizations competing in multiple markets should organize their business units, wherever possible, with managerial authority over all required mainstream business functions. Where not possible—due to critical mass, rapidly shifting markets, and so forth—they need to approximate fully authorized business teams with whatever compensatory mechanisms are available.

Manager of Many Resources

To be genuinely accountable for the overall results of a business, one must also have sufficient authority (as defined previously) over those functions that assist in defining, obtaining, allocating, and improving the resources necessary to conduct business. The three categories of resources required to run a business are:

1. Capital.
2. People.
3. Processes.

This defines the necessary business-unit "resourcing" functions: financial (analysis), human resources, and process improvement.

One of the perpetual pendulum movements we observe in industry is the swing every several years from centralizing to decentralizing "resourcing" functions between corporate and individual business units. The assumption partially underlying these shifts is that these types of functions are either necessary for control or are ancillary services. Corporate finds itself unable to control maverick BU heads, so it decides to rein them in by establishing a direct line with the BU heads' "resourcing" functions. Or corporate decides the functions are merely "overhead," so it outsources them entirely. The logic here in both cases is that these functions are not integral to the direct running of the business or to the continuous improvement of business thinking.

Neither is true. When properly structured, defined, and filled, "resourcing" roles are absolutely critical to the planning, modeling, adjusting, and coordinating of many aspects of the business. I view the primary purpose of these "resourcing" functions as helping the accountable BU head to translate his business concept into alternative resource models. The presentation of the model might sound like this: "If we want this much cash flow and this level of EBITDA, we could emphasize either this marketing thrust or that development investment or X, Y, or Z. The first model would require this amount of capital, allocated across our business functions in this way, and that a new type of employee skill set and a certain type of technology change. The second model would require the following adjustments in the resource mix...."

When these functions are centralized corporately, they become more oriented toward controlling BU activity. The proper means for addressing maverick business-unit heads or inconsistently implemented systems and processes is through system stewardship, not centralization of strategic "resourcing" functions (more on system stewardship later in the chapter).

When they are centralized into a resource pool for economies of scale, they tend to be viewed as a service, focused mainly on minimizing cost rather than being directly connected to the BU head's thinking and adding value to her total business modeling on an ongoing basis.

Taking Care of Business

In addition, to meet his accountabilities for delivering on the overall business results, the business-unit head must have sufficient authority over *stewardship functions*. These functions support the BU head in ensuring that all of his resources are *used as intended, fully accounted for,* and *cared for properly.* Stewardship functions, for the same three types of resources, tend to be called financial control and audit; environment, health, and safety; and quality assurance.

It is important to understand how fundamentally different the focus of the "resourcing" functions is from the stewardship functions.

Financial analysis, for instance, should be primarily focused on developing what-if scenarios for the BU head and mainstream functions. Financial control, on the other hand, should be focused on the gap between what is and what was agreed upon. Individuals in "resourcing" functions model the optimization of resource allocation and capability. They tend to ask questions such as, "What is the best way to adjust Plan B to capitalize on every opportunity?" Individuals in stewardship functions support the adherence to the existing plans in order to ensure a focused, disciplined implementation of strategy. They prod others by making statements such as, "Let's make sure that if we deviate from Plan B, we do so on purpose, not by default or neglect." The orientation of each of these two categories of functions requires different skills and different mindsets.

The structural implication of this reality is that stewardship functions, like "resourcing" functions, should be directly subordinated to BU heads given enough critical mass. These functions should not be centralized corporately. Furthermore, if possible, one should consider separating financial analysis from financial control to ensure the proper tension between these competing forces. A real danger occurs when "resourcing" and stewardship functions are combined, because any particular discipline head (finance, HR, process improvement) will tend to value and emphasize one type of function to the detriment of the other.

Mighty Fighting SBUs

Now, we can begin to model a business unit using three of the building blocks of structural design. Elliott Jaques discovered empirically that large corporations and governmental hierarchies prosper when they organize their major trading or fighting units at a particular size—that is, at a predictable level of role complexity. Take a look at the following graphic (Levels of Role Complexity).

In particular, he found, after a decade-long period of research for the U.S. Army, that the largest whole fighting units (ones that can be deployed and redeployed into various theaters of battle without being broken up) are divisions. He also found that a division two-star general is a Level-5 role. Jaques further discovered that this pattern of Level-5 divisions repeated itself in all combat-ready armies in the world. When lives and the fate of nations are at stake, one can assume rigorous "field testing" of this architecture has occurred over the centuries. And in fact, whenever armies have deviated from this architecture during the course of history, their casualties escalated and their effectiveness declined dramatically.

If we think of doing business as engaging in economic warfare in a free-market economy, we can extrapolate from this knowledge about the ideal size for most P&L business units. Businesses, trading in defined marketplaces with defined ranges of products, services, and technologies, are optimally Level-5 entities.

In order to align structure with strategy, the design issue for creating business units at the proper level hinges on the following competing dilemmas:

- The higher the organizational level where true P&L accountability first occurs, the more complex the task of deciding on functional resource allocations to multiple groups doing business in multiple markets.
- The lower the level of initial P&L accountability, the more complex the task of integrating each BU's products and services into larger deliverables that require many BUs to produce.

System Stewardship: Nested Direct-and-Indirect Accountabilities

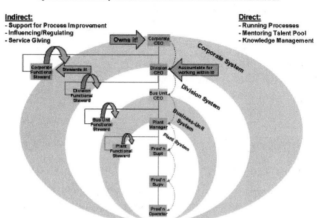

In order to resolve this impasse, I have found that the following sequence of six activities should be followed:

1. Identify the organizing logic and critical success factors—derived from strategy—that define the necessary BU mainstream functions.
2. Choose the logic around which Level-5 strategic business units (SBUs) will be created.
3. Identify the necessary mainstream, "resourcing," stewardship, and ancillary-service roles to support the accountable SBU head.
4. Identify the interbusiness-unit and intrabusiness-unit synergies to be supported by cross-functional working relationships.
5. Align the corporate specialist functions with the corporate SBU and business-development functions.
6. Establish the appropriate system-stewardship roles at each level of management and their working relationships with other roles in the organization.

The Final Piece of the Puzzle

A key stumbling block in the quest for unambiguous, reality-based managerial accountability is eliminating the need for matrix management relationships—the ubiquitous straight-and-dotted-line managers.

In Chapter 8, I focused on a way to ensure vital cross-functional processes—processes that are simultaneously accountable, capable, and efficient. I described three categories of indirect accountabilities where roles had lateral accountabilities in relation to other roles to support them in meeting their own direct accountabilities for process outputs.

As you'll recall, these indirect accountabilities consisted of support for process improvement (in relation to process-accountable managers), service-giving, and influencing and regulating accountabilities (such as informing, persuading, and instructing others regarding their judgments and actions).

How often have you seen a line manager deliver on his accountabilities for ambitious targets, but at the expense of violating critical process or system requirements? How often do you hear from the CFO or director of safety and health or the VP of corporate marketing that he is unable to meet his accountabilities because of all the cowboys in the business units who insist on managing processes *their* way? Or conversely, how often do BU heads complain that the so-called staff functions have too much power and that they are nothing more than officious bureaucrats who live to say "no"?

This internal competition for control is often viewed as a necessary evil in large organizations and is the justification for establishing multiple-boss systems. Because the CEO cannot get his division COO's BU heads to behave, he tells his CFO to manage the BU controllers and tame the business units through the back door.

At the root of this inefficient and conflict-producing approach is a combination of managerial abdication and inadequate knowledge of system stewardship. *The CEO must hold his COO accountable for ensuring that each of his BU heads runs his or her businesses within the requirements of all corporate systems.* This is a fundamental managerial accountability. Failure to do so should not be treated merely as a sign of ineffectiveness; it should also be viewed as insubordination.

With this accountability leadership mindset, managers get religion in a hurry! They immediately realize that ignoring the systems' requirements will not only affect their pay, but it will also have a strong impact on their career and continued employment. The difficulty in sustaining this tension, however, is that managers often do not have the time, the technical expertise, or the means for personally ensuring system adherence by their subordinates. Here is where the concept of *system stewardship* (see the preceding graphic) comes into play.

The process-accountable manager, who "owns" a particular system, needs to delegate system stewardship accountability to one subordinate, who then has a combination of direct and indirect accountabilities. The *indirect* accountabilities are most visible, require active vigilance and interaction laterally, and typically constitute all three types of indirect working relationships. None of these requires managerial authority over people lateral to them in the organization, but they all involve making judgments about the thinking, decisions, and actions of others, and about the integrity of the processes themselves. In this way, the need for straight- and dotted-line manager solutions can be completely eliminated. Instead, as you saw in Chapter 8, accountability leadership offers a far more precise and accurate way to address lateral accountabilities for systems.

System stewardship may also require some *direct* accountabilities for processes, usually for running process infrastructures but not for delivering the process outputs themselves. It may also carry direct accountabilities for resource modeling for a function as part of a strategic-planning initiative. Finally, system stewardship has recently been given direct accountability for the management of proprietary knowledge as well as industry-specific knowledge about the functions underpinning the system.

In Chapters 7 and 8, we examined the role that manager-subordinate teams and three-level process units play in extending accountability from a vertical A-B-C managerial process into a series of lateral accountabilities, all in relation to a process-accountable manager. In this chapter, we filled out the four building blocks for aligning larger structures with strategy: levels, functions, process, and systems.

In Chapter 10, we will build upon the development concepts presented in Chapter 6 and look at a systematic method for aligning people with structure today, tomorrow, and in the strategic future.

---

[1] As in *Requisite Organization,* Part 3, Section 2, on functional alignment.

Chapter 10
Developing a Talent-Pool System

Mitch Sumner, the CEO of a multi-billion dollar supplier to the aerospace industry, was facing a serious challenge. He was three years away from retirement, and both he and Nigel Ogilvy, the chairman of the European-parent company, were worried about succession. Although extremely profitable, this U.S. division had focused so much on acquisitions, production performance, and sales during the past decade that the company had ignored the development needs of its managerial talent pool.

Now Mitch and Nigel found themselves in an unenviable position. More than 60 percent of their top 50 executives had to retire within five years and no effective plan had been developed for their replacement. Mitch had two younger executives he had been informally grooming for the CEO position, but neither he nor Nigel was comfortable that they were ready. And they could not quite figure out why.

A high-level task force of operational and HR executives explored various alternative ways to assess and develop the company's talent pool. They found a thriving industry of assessment companies that offered to put scores, if not hundreds, of its managers through exhaustive (and expensive) competency exams. These companies promised sophisticated profiles of the executives' strengths and weaknesses, high-level executive coaching, and detailed development plans. They were, in short, offering to allow the company's managers to abdicate even further their accountabilities for developing their people.

Fortunately, this type of shortcut did not sit well with the task force. The company had always prided itself in figuring out what it needed to do to remain competitive. It was not afraid of hard work or of holding its managers accountable for doing what was necessary. The company just did not know where or how to begin systematically appraising its current pool of talent. It was not even sure what to assess or against what standards they needed to develop its people. But the task force pushed on, looking for knowledge and practical applications that would equip their own managers with the skills and a system to get the company's pipelines filled with capable people able to support its business strategy.

I had previously worked with the company on an unrelated organizational-design project. Mitch approached The Levinson Institute again at this time because of our principle-based, scientific approach to developing leadership systems. I explained the fundamentals of human potential and other capabilities and their relationship to the levels of role complexity. I demonstrated a straightforward and easy-to-implement approach to educating and assisting all managers in the accurate assessment of employee potential (current and future), effectiveness in current role, and developmental needs. The company saw how this approach (concepts, education, assessment, and development) could be effectively and accountably implemented and how it could, in addition, significantly improve the accuracy of its selection and recruitment processes.

After several months of working with the senior executive team, educating and helping them to assess their next two levels of managers, I sat down with Mitch and Larry Goodson, his VP of HR. We examined a potential-pipeline map developed by the executive team and looked for possible successors to the CEO. Surprisingly, the one manager who would possess the raw potential in three years to handle the U.S. CEO position—a high Level-6 role—was a senior technologist in one of their business units. He was not very well-known to top management. Furthermore, although this individual was extremely effective in his current role, he had little commercial and no actual manufacturing experience. (His manager had recently begun a developmental plan to equip him to become a business-unit head in six or seven years.)

The two other managers who had been viewed as possible successors were, indeed, on the map, but they were judged not likely to mature into high Level-6 potential for at least another seven to eight years. Both of them were considered extremely strong candidates for the CEO position *at that time*. Based on this overview, Mitch asked Larry to initiate a recruitment search immediately for a high-level executive from the industry with current high Level-6 potential (or higher) in his or her mid-fifties. In this way, he would have three years to learn the ropes of this company and another five to seven years in the role until he retired—exactly at the right time for one of the two younger managers to move into the top position.

The process was so successful in helping to make these key decisions covering the next five years that Mitch decided to accelerate and broaden the process of its subsequent implementation to cover not only all managers, but also all 8,000 U.S. employees.

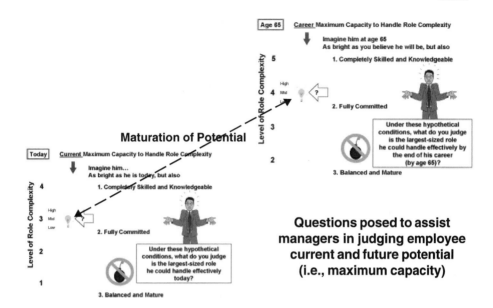

Questions posed to assist managers in judging employee current and future potential (i.e., maximum capacity)

Speaking of Potential

As you'll remember from Chapter 6, potential is one of the most poorly understood aspects of human capability, even in those organizations that devote a lot of time and energy to succession planning. Potential to do what? Potential to fill a particular role today? In five years? In 10 years? Never?

Potential, in the way I am defining it, is *the raw capacity to handle complexity.* It is innate and it matures biologically over an individual's entire adult lifetime. Potential exists independently of knowledge and skill acquired from experience and training. Potential exists independently of commitment and emotional maturity. Put another way, potential refers to how large a role someone *could* handle if he or she were to acquire the knowledge, value the work, and function maturely at a particular level.

In *Human Capability*[1], Elliott Jaques and Kathryn Cason report the findings of their groundbreaking research about potential. They demonstrate convincingly that a specific line (see the following graphic) of questioning yields not only *reliable* appraisals of employee current potential (that is, strong agreement between employee, manager, and skip-level manager), but also *valid* conclusions when compared with the complexity of the employee's mental processing.

Maturation of Potential

Is this employee in these pictures big enough for the position he is already in? At what level is this role? Is he fully effective in this current position? If not, what is

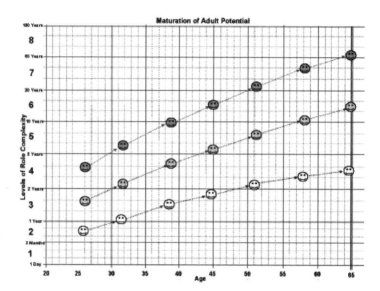

he lacking? Knowledge? Skill? Commitment? Maturity? If he were to fill in those gaps, could he fully master this position? Could he handle an even bigger role today under the right conditions? How big and under what conditions? What, therefore, is his raw potential or horsepower right now?

As you can see, although this is a straightforward line of reasoning, it is not a precise measurement. It requires judgment—actually many judgments—to evaluate the multiple factors that account for how well an individual currently functions in a role and the sense that one gets about how well he *could* function in other larger roles. The good news is that the assessment system yields not only accurate judgments of potential, but it also heightens managerial awareness about the gaps between an employee's actual effectiveness and potential effectiveness. This gap analysis becomes the basis for accurate and effective managerial coaching of employees to increase the value they add in their roles.

What Happens Next?

One of the most startling empirical findings made by Elliott Jaques is a pattern of predictable rates of maturation of potential for all adults: He found that by judging an individual's current potential and then reassessing that individual every five to 10 years, each adult's potential or mental capacity grew at a predictable rate similar to those of other biological processes. The graph above depicts this idea visually.

This finding, validated by Dr. Jaques following over 40 years of research, is often difficult for people to accept, for it challenges three strongly held beliefs:

1. The beloved Horatio Alger myth that anyone who is strongly enough motivated can achieve anything he or she wants to through hard work, courage, and tenacity. This is simply not true, although diligence *will* probably increase the likelihood that someone will more fully realize his or her *innate* potential.

2. The notion that people who progress in their careers become more capable because of their experience, training, and on-the-job mastery. Although this is true in one sense—greater skilled knowledge and focus will definitely increase one's effectiveness—it is not true in another sense. Experience will not increase one's potential effectiveness. That effectiveness will mature naturally over time.

3. The belief that expectations strongly determine potential, so that judging someone's potential and communicating that assessment to him is a dangerous thing to do. There is certainly ample evidence that expectations influence a person's self-image and self-confidence. Not recognizing or underestimating someone's actual potential may, indeed, result in loss of confidence and yield diminished performance (that is, a widening of the gap between his potential and actual effectiveness). On the other hand, accurately recognizing an individual's potential may enhance his motivation to realize that potential and improve performance (that is, narrowing the gap). There is, however, no evidence that communicating someone's potential to him will have any impact at all on the expected rate of normal maturation of that potential.

Most people accept the fact that every individual is born with the potential to grow to a certain height that is genetically predetermined. Diet and illness may interfere with an individual's actual physical growth, but her ultimate height was determined before birth. We also expect that girls will achieve their ultimate "vertical" potential in their mid-teens and boys in their late-teens or early 20s.

When we stop to realize that the modern human brain is a comparatively recent evolutionary development and is much more complicated than the musculo-skeletal-endocrine system, then 60 to 80 years for full brain maturation versus 20 years for full skeletal growth is not that great a leap of faith.

The ultimate question is whether this new knowledge about maturation of potential is consistent with the way managers in business organizations actually think about their people and whether building a system using this knowledge can improve upon an organization's management of its pipelines of potential.

Mapping Pipelines of Potential

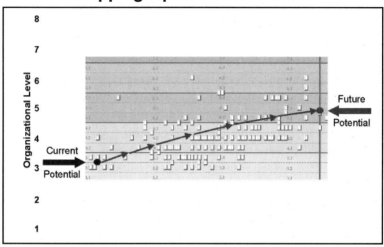

Big-Tent Evaluations

Imagine sitting down with an HR specialist after having determined how your organization's roles fit into the underlying pattern of complexity levels and after developing the "mental models" of types of work complexity and types of mental complexity. Then, imagine posing the hypothetical questions previously enumerated about each of your immediate subordinates and their subordinates.

If you were to place a notation for each individual's current potential on a chart at the appropriate level, you could then compare individuals with each other *with respect to their current raw abilities*—not their current performance. Although awkward at the beginning, managers soon get the knack of looking beyond their subordinates' overall effectiveness and zeroing in on their current potential. See the graphic above.

Next, imagine looking at those people whose current maximum capacity (CMC) places them within a particular maturation pipeline and comparing individuals at one age-CMC point with other individuals in the same pipeline at other age-CMC points. Can you envision that an individual at one point in a pipeline will likely have the same CMC in 10 years that another individual, who is currently 10 years older, has today?

Or conversely, can you envision that this individual had the same CMC 10 years ago that another individual, who is 10 years younger and in the same pipeline, has today? When you compare individuals against each other with respect to their *mode of potential maturation* (that is, their maturation pipeline), you are really judging whether they were "cast from the same mold" or "cut from the same cloth." Ultimately, this process helps managers to sharpen their focus and accuracy in asking, "How high in the organization do I judge this individual will eventually have the problem-solving ability to function?" You are not assessing how *likely* it is that the individual will actually achieve that level of promotion. Rather, you are assessing whether you believe he or she has the potential, by career end, to handle work of a certain level of complexity.

Once you complete this process for all of your immediate subordinates and subordinates-once-removed, you will then participate in a group "gearing" session with your manager and his other subordinates.[1] During this eye-opening meeting, the group of you will be guided through a systematic reevaluation of the initial judgments about the entire group of employees two and three levels below your manager.

This big-tent evaluation is critical for several reasons. First is the reality that these assessments constitute judgments, not measurements, of potential. The accuracy of these judgments hinges on many things, including the degree to which the levels of complexity are accurately understood and the degree to which individual biases about specific employees or groups of employees can be minimized. Open, honest, and direct communication in an executive team helps to facilitate both of these goals. What results from a well-led gearing session are a reliable model, a common language, and a powerful standard for assessing role size and human capability.

Another reason that the evaluation is critical is the learning that occurs during these discussions by managers about their own people when getting feedback about them from their peers. It is precisely during these gearing sessions that managers begin to fill in their understanding of their people and learn to evaluate the four factors determining their effectiveness: raw potential, skilled knowledge, commitment, and maturity. In their minds, managers must separate potential effectiveness from actual effectiveness; the gearing process provides them with a framework and a discipline to do so.

A third reason is the building of a knowledgeable and engaged group of senior managers who thoroughly understands the ingredients of its organization's talent pool. Each manager participating in this gearing process gets a more accurate view of the current state of the company's pipelines of potential and begins to feel a greater sense of personal ownership over the system of development. In addition, each feels more confident in knowing what to communicate to immediate subordinates in coaching sessions and to subordinates-once-removed in mentoring sessions. This translates into a greater sense of competence and mastery in the developmental aspects of their roles. Many managers come to value this work, when previously it made them feel inadequate.

What is missing from this discussion is the importance of a deep-and-broad experience in ensuring the proper design and implementation of this talent-pool-development system, especially over the first year. I have attempted to explain and describe the process for the reader to evaluate its logic and ability to leverage human potential. I would strongly urge leaders considering implementing such an approach to engage seasoned experts with years of experience with the concepts and tools.

An Exciting New Development

You'll recall the processes of coaching and mentoring from Chapter 6. Coaching is logically the accountability of an employee's immediate manager, because the managerial role is accountable both for ensuring employee effectiveness and enhancing it. Mentoring is logically the accountability of an employee's manager-once-removed, because that role should be accountable for ensuring a capable pool of employees from which to fill future subordinate-level positions.[2]

In every managerial leadership system, the CEO is accountable for having a talent pool–development system, with which to meet his overall commitments to the board of directors for having capable people to deliver on the company's strategy. The VP of HR is usually accountable for stewarding the talent pool–development system on behalf of the CEO, to ensure that the system is operated consistently throughout the organization, that necessary services (which require specialized skills and processes) are given, and that the development processes themselves are continuously improved.

We have now come full circle in this approach to the D part of LEAD: development. The very nature of managerial leadership systems is that they are accountability hierarchies. This accountability cascades down the organization (Managers A, B, and C) not only around assignments and limits, but also around stewardship of resources. The CEO must steward human resources *locally* by appraising subordinate effectiveness and coaching to enhance it and by appraising subordinate-once-removed potential and mentoring to help realize it. The CEO must also steward human resources *globally* by ensuring a system of recruitment, assessment, development, selection, compensation, and retention. Similarly, every manager has local people-development accountabilities and all managers at Level 3 and higher must steward their own people-development *subsystems*.

By now, this process should seem perfectly logical and sensible to you—a win-win situation for everyone. However, there are very few organizations around the world that have implemented approaches such as these as systemically and systematically as described. Why not? What are the four most common barriers to such an employee-commitment-engaging and employee-capability-enhancing process?

- The general confusion that exists in the field of organizational development about what potential is and what development of potential really requires.
- The more pervasive absence of universally applied managerial accountability.
- The specific confusion created in most matrix approaches to management about who is really accountable for assessment, coaching, and mentoring.
- A simple lack of will and the resulting lack of focus about an organization-wide system for development.

To help alleviate these barriers, The Levinson Institute has recently developed software called LEO that greatly simplifies the implementation and management of a talent pool–development system. In addition, the software provides a valuable tool for proactive HR-pipeline modeling and succession planning. When combined with all of the elements described in this chapter, LEO turns strategically aligned human-resource development into a distinct competitive advantage and a powerful lever to attract and retain top talent.

Make a Strategic Selection!

Let's say you work for a multinational corporation. Your company has implemented a talent pool–development system. You need to fill an important mid-level vacant position, a low Level-4 plant-manager position directly subordinate to you.

You ask *your* manager and the appropriate HR specialist to run the following search using the LEO talent pool–development software:

1. Find all employees worldwide judged to have CMC (current maximum capacity) of low Level 4 or higher (that is, those with sufficient raw ability).
2. Select from that pool a subgroup currently employed in roles with LoRC (level of role complexity) of low Level 4 or lower (that is, those for whom this selection would represent a promotion or lateral developmental transfer).
3. Identify among that next subgroup those who have, along with their manager-once-removed, identified a role of this nature as a desirable next step in their development (that is, those for whom this role is feasible and desirable in terms of work valued).
4. Explore within that smaller pool which employees in Level-4 roles have a DEA (demonstrated effectiveness appraisal) of 3 or higher

and which employees in Level-3 roles have a DEA of 5 or higher (that is, those who have demonstrated strong commitment and already deliver a high level of value).

5. Drill down into that narrowing slate of potential candidates and match each individual's current inventory of skilled knowledge and types of work valued against the profile of the role you are trying to fill. How effective is this individual likely to be early on in this new role?

6. Identify from this near final slate of candidates those with ratings of dysfunction greater than -1 and track their progress in improving on those behaviors.

7. Screen this group against any specifically defined organizational development and/or EEO needs (that is, those people who are key players in the future who need to be fast tracked, those from departments or geographies needing more development, or those people who would help the company meet some of its diversity objectives).

8. Finally, see whether this role would represent a good opportunity to recruit a mid- to senior-level person from the outside to fill an identified gap in the potential pipeline. Put another way, should the selection be made from within or is this too important an opportunity not to recruit high-level talent from outside the company?

Given the slate of candidates that comes from this search, you then decide which individuals will best fill the role's requirements. (This is explained visually in the HR Modeling: Selection graphic on the next page.) Keep in mind that a selecting manager does not need the authority to select *anyone* in the company he chooses. However, the selecting manager should have the authority, when presented with a list of appropriate candidates, to choose that individual he feels can best do the job.

These eight questions bring an unprecedented level of specificity and accuracy to talent-pool development. This accountability leadership approach allows for the optimal balancing of multiple, competing, yet legitimate needs from many different parts of an organization. The methodology increases the likelihood of accurate role-filling decisions and optimal developmental requirements.

You have now experienced all of the elements of LEAD: leveraging potential, engaging commitment, aligning judgment, and developing capability. You have

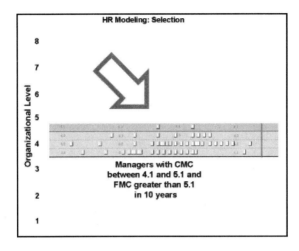

explored the basic underlying principles of each in Part II and their practical applications so far in Part III. What remains is an exploration of the role of leadership in defining, communicating, and engaging an organization effectively around the many changes required to fully implement accountability leadership.

In Chapter 11, we conclude the Accountability Leadership adventure by defining the meaning and the requirements of adaptive leadership.

---

[1]Elliott Jaques and Kathryn Cason, *Human Capability.*

[2]The concept that the manager-once-removed should be the accountable mentor is a significant part of Jaques's talent-pool-development process.

Chapter 11
Adaptive Leadership

Remember the two machine operators from the beginning of Chapter 4? They described their vastly different perspectives on the changes Mr. Petro initiated in his company. The first operator felt betrayed. The second operator felt vindicated, relieved, and extremely positive about the company and its future.

How can two people, working together in the same company and undergoing the same organizational transformation, experience things so differently? It has everything to do with the changing psychological contract and what I call a culture of adaptive readiness.

Employees in Mr. Petro's company who were comfortable and pleased with the existing contract, lasting more than a generation and supporting an attitude of employee entitlement, were angered with a change based upon accountability leadership. Those who were dismayed by the danger previous management had placed the company in welcomed the change. But no matter where people stand, change always represents loss coupled with new demands. And that amounts to a violation of the psychological contract.

Wise leaders understand the importance of communicating change and renegotiating the psychological contract.

Adapting to Change

All living organisms struggle for survival and mastery in relationship to their environments. The process of struggling and succeeding is called adaptation. Many people think of adaptation as simply adjusting or coping, but at its core, adaptation is really about increasing one's competitive advantage in relationship to the environment. This is true for microorganisms, for butterflies, for elephants, and for humans. It is also true for businesses and for nations. The ultimate goal of any business organization is to fulfill its underlying purpose and to perpetuate itself by continuously adapting to the requirements of the marketplace.

The developments in human evolution that account for our greater adaptive capacity in relation to lower-order animals boil down to four uniquely human capabilities:

- Cognition. The ability to process data, to create new information, to project future scenarios, and to develop novel solutions for them.
- Communication. The ability to convey such newly developed information to others, using articulated language, and thereby enhance their knowledge.
- Mobilization. The ability to convert emotions into values, to craft goals—in common with others—based on these values, and to engage individual and collective commitment to deliver on those goals.
- Invention. The ability to create new tools and access information for solving problems and overcoming obstacles.

If you think carefully about these basic properties of human ingenuity, you can see that they explain the force underlying the power of LEAD.

Managerial leaders add value to their subordinates (and to the organization as a whole) by:

- Processing complexity at a level higher than their subordinates and using that capability to *leverage* subordinate potential.
- Communicating their aspirations and passions in order to *engage* subordinate commitment.
- Communicating intentions and means for achieving them, in order to *align* subordinate judgment and discretion.
- Developing resources and subordinate capabilities to support their realizing their potential and meeting their accountabilities.

Leadership, in other words, is the ultimate manifestation of human adaptive capacity. It is the primary process in modern society where human potential is fully realized. And it is the force necessary to create a culture of adaptive readiness in organizations.

At the core of adaptation is an organization's ability to respond to, or anticipate, changes in the environment in such a way as to increase its leverage over the environment. But critical change carries with it tremendous vulnerability, for failure to adapt to this change means defeat. The Chinese people understood this double-edged sword eons ago when they created the word for crisis: we che.

Inherent in all critical change is a threat to survival if new demands are not met as well as an opportunity to prosper if the new demands are mastered. The way in which leaders present new change realities to their people, equip them

We Che

Crisis = Danger + Opportunity

to address those realities, and support them in learning and growing will determine whether those people will become optimists or pessimists about future change. Leaders can help their people master the new demands and come to realize that through change they can better realize their potential. Demonstrating this creates a culture that not only welcomes but also seeks out change. When employees are actively engaged in scouring the environment for opportunities to improve an organization's competitive advantage, that company has created a *culture of adaptive readiness.*

To Every Thing There Is a Season

Dr. Harry Levinson's formulation of the psychological contract[1] has been a major advance in understanding the force underlying employee identification with, and commitment to, an organization's leadership. He was also one of the earliest researchers to identify the sources of resistance to change and the nature of managerial leverage in overcoming that resistance.

Think of the way people form attachments in their lives as being similar to the way a tree puts down roots. Roots are necessary to anchor a tree. Similarly, every individual is rooted in multiple attachments, from which she derives identity and draws emotional and intellectual sustenance. The graphic on page 158 depicts some of these roots.

People come to depend on these attachments not only for a sense of permanence, but also for their sense of self. So, when a significant attachment is threatened, either in a physical or a symbolic way, whether or not the threat is real or imagined, people recoil and turn inward. Dr. Levinson summarized it elegantly: *All change is loss—the loss of what has been*[2].

A critical change is a major impact, a threat, or a departure from the status quo. It immediately poses two types of threats to an individual's emotional, behavioral, and productive equilibrium: loss and new demands. Think of the uprooting as loss: loss of being anchored, loss of identity and familiarity, loss of control, loss of support, and loss of confidence and competence. Coping with loss consumes physical, intellectual, and emotional energy.

Attachments and Change
Roots of Identification

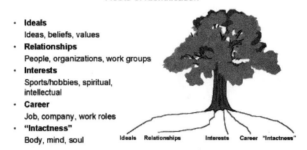

- **Ideals**
  Ideas, beliefs, values
- **Relationships**
  People, organizations, work groups
- **Interests**
  Sports/hobbies, spiritual,
  intellectual
- **Career**
  Job, company, work roles
- **"Intactness"**
  Body, mind, soul

Ideals   Relationships   Interests   Career   "Intactness"

Our identities are "rooted" in multiple
real, as well as abstract, attachments.

In order to free up that energy, managers need to help people carefully examine the meanings they have assigned to that severed attachment. Preserve the good things that can continue. Retain the good memories about good things that cannot continue. Celebrate the loss of bad things. This is, in essence, a kind of mourning.

Adaptive leaders help people to acknowledge the losses inherent in the changes they must contend with. Exercising this leverage helps to restore confidence in leadership and begins the process of renegotiating the psychological contract.

The second type of threat to an individual's equilibrium comes from the new demands inherent in forming new roots. We all struggle with feelings of inadequacy, which are perfectly human but painful nevertheless. Any time someone has to "start from scratch," which is what critical change foists upon him, he is filled with dread about being awkward, appearing ridiculous, and ultimately failing to meet the requirements of new demands.

Managers need to recognize the anxiety, fear, and stress that coping with these new demands places on their people—that this aspect of change also consumes considerable energy, requiring active managerial support. Leaders need to frame for their employees that the process of change is experimenting with new ways of thinking and performing and that experiments are really calculated risks—a kind of trial and error. Taking a reasonable, albeit radically new approach is healthy, and an outcome other than the one intended should not be considered a mistake but rather a valuable point of learning. By helping people to get excited about learning, inventing, and creating, leaders create opportunities for growth and mastery. They help their people to get a better feel for their own potential and how gratifying it can be to realize it.

Leaders need to see themselves as transitional anchors: sources of attachment during the transition from which their people can draw acknowledgement, support, encouragement, resources, information, and confidence. Managers need not be

Critical Change Sequence

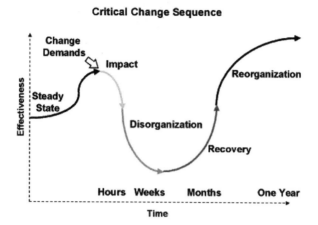

omniscient in order to serve as effective anchors. However, they need to be available, attentive, and aware. They need to maintain perspective about the transition, its dangers and opportunities, and its stages and pitfalls. Managers also need to help renegotiate the fractured psychological contracts.

It's Going to Be a Bumpy Night

Each phase of critical change (illustrated above) carries its own demands on the people going through it. The initial impact is usually somewhat shocking. When people first register a major change in their immediate environment and working conditions, their initial response is to feel overwhelmed. They simply cannot comprehend the enormity of what it will mean for them. For seconds, minutes, or even hours, people will exist in a state of suspended disbelief. They focus neither on the past nor on the future.

In order to avoid this kind of shock, managers should be setting context on an ongoing basis about anticipated changes so that people will be better prepared for whatever develops. But when managers must convey unexpected and potentially traumatic information to people, they should remember that people will begin to tune out after a few sentences of bad news—once the enormity is registered. Thus it is necessary to carefully script a concise, to-the-point message to be delivered simply and briefly. It should be followed up later with doses of detail, as people begin to assimilate new information.

Once the reality sets in, the second phase of critical change, disorganization, typically begins. Think of this period as a chaotic unleashing of unproductive energy. It can be understood as a state of heightened alarm, with thoughts and emotions racing and the body's fight-flight adrenaline response on red alert. People feel quite ill at ease, anxious, and fearful.

This phase poses extreme challenges for managers, because they need to ensure that their people focus on doing their day-to-day work while also focusing on understanding, formulating, and implementing new ways of doing things—during a time when they are less able to focus well on anything! Compounding this are the universal feelings among most employees during critical change: mistrust in, and betrayal by, their managers.

This is a critical time for leaders to act as anchors. They must speak with authoritative reassurance that the changes are real but that they are manageable. Leaders need to address reality and simultaneously provide confidence.

People often swing between being impulsive and indecisive. This also requires more forceful direction than a leader would normally display. It is equally important to give people as much information and control as is practical in order to combat the normal feelings of helplessness during a crisis. During this phase, managers need to support multiple forums for people to talk about the change: to acquire information, to quell rumors, to clarify meanings, and to receive encouragement.

During this phase, people tend to focus on themselves. "What will happen to *me*?" they worry. The focus is on what they had before and how they might recapture the old way of doing things. Energy is quickly depleted from dealing with the present and planning for the future. This phase ends when people tire of worrying and complaining, when they accept the reality of the loss, and when they have confidence that their leader will help them to succeed in mastering the new demands. If well managed, this phase should merge into the next phase in one to two months as people begin to shift their focus from the past to the present tasks at hand.

The third phase of critical change, recovery, now begins. This is a period of experimentation, where people struggle to keep afloat in treacherous and uncharted waters. They are often hesitant, insecure, and afraid of failing. Managers need to be less directive and more Socratic, drawing out their subordinates' thinking about a problem and constructing a solution. Leaders must give their employees opportunities to try out new ways of working without knowing ahead of time if they will succeed. They must encourage risks without allowing recklessness. This is a time to help people find early successes in order to build confidence and momentum. It is vital to provide accurate, objective, and immediate feedback to ensure genuine learning. It is equally important to provide encouragement and praise for well-designed and executed plans.

Depending on the degree of change required and the amount and effectiveness of support given to employees, this phase may last another three-to-six months. The hope is to see people functioning reasonably well in their newly defined roles and accomplishing many aspects of the new processes by this time. They will have recovered much confidence in themselves and in the organization and its leaders, but they are not yet fully acclimated to the new ways of doing things. Maintaining the gains still requires a conscious effort and some emotional expenditure. At the point of transitioning into the final phase, people begin to look forward to the future.

The fourth phase of critical change is reorganization. During the next six months, people attempt to assimilate their new skills, knowledge, and new working relationships.

It is during this phase that managerial leaders, who have earned the trust, respect, and confidence of their people in the previous phases, can exert the final leverage toward building a new culture with a renegotiated psychological contract. This requires a great deal of communication, but of a different sort than before. People need time to reflect on their journey, celebrate their successes, anchor their learning, and contemplate on how much more adaptive they have proven themselves to be. In this manner, leaders can instill and reinforce a hunger for learning, for growth, and for mastery. They can point to the evidence of their employees' potential to move the organization forward, when each understands better his own potential, his own accountabilities and authorities, and his role in supporting the whole team (and the organization) to survive and thrive.

Successfully Leading Change

The implementation of accountability leadership in any managerial system takes time, focus, consistency, and commitment. For most organizations, it requires a significant adjustment in its culture. It needs to go from one based primarily on personal responsibility to one built on a foundation of accountability.

This transformation will inevitably create tremendous tension and uncertainty for the people undergoing it before it is successfully implemented. Some of the strain will be due to the significant shift in paradigm and in required behaviors. However, as we have seen, some upheaval is due to the process of change itself.

From years of consultation and observation, I have found that the best organizational leaders do several specific things to successfully implement organizational change:

- They communicate and provide information so that people will understand that the change is both necessary and reasonable.
- They provide clarification about the implications of the change decision in order to encourage trust. (No surprises!)
- They model behavior so that there will be greater identification with the boss, with management, and with new organizational goals.
- They seek input and advice so that people will remain genuinely committed and support the change.

- They set limits to encourage appropriate behavior and mutual respect.

Similarly, the effectiveness of the organizational change implementation itself will depend on four closely related variables:

1. Obviously, the plan needs to be a good plan. It must apply the essential principles of LEAD, ensuring that structure and process are fully aligned with strategy, that accountabilities are clear and fully aligned with authorities, and that people are accurately aligned with the requirements of their roles.

2. The people who will implement the plan must come to accept that the plan is necessary, good, and reasonable.

3. The people who will implement the plan must come to a point of personal ownership of the plan. They need to be convinced it will help them to succeed.

4. Managers must set clear limits around what is acceptable and desirable behavior by employees during the change.

During times of change the leader's credo sometimes becomes, "You may not like these changes, but you must work and act constructively to support them."

Implementing Accountability Leadership

By now, you have learned about organizational physics. You have explored leadership-system-engineering principles. Now, how do you effect change and successfully implement accountability leadership in your organization? Carefully, deliberately, seriously, knowledgeably, confidently, and consistently!

Part of this book's premise is that most current organizations function like a camel that intended to be a horse but was designed by a committee: blindfolded. Every element of a managerial leadership system is intimately tied to every other element. Nature intends for it to operate seamlessly—accountably, capably, and efficiently—just as the human body does. Because most existing knowledge of leadership, structure, process, and HR systems is based on undefined, ill-defined, or untested premises, most organizations are mired in slogans and groundless theories.

I fervently believe that leaders who undertake accountability leadership will be able to use LEAD as a competitive weapon. However, implementing accountability leadership requires the same diligence that every other strategic function and technology requires.

LEAD: From Strategy to Structure

First comes the word from on high. People need to have clear communication from the CEO and senior management about what is being undertaken, why, at what cost, at what pace, and within what boundary conditions. This is especially critical given the level of cynicism that exists in most companies about various management fads of the month. Remember that accountability leadership transcends fads.

As with any engineering redesign process, one needs to start by accurately clarifying and defining the current state of affairs. This is what I call the *actual* organization. This picture is constructed from three kinds of data:

- The overt organization (that is, the organization chart).
- The covert organization or the informal, responsibility processes.
- The role and process analyses (cascading interviews from the CEO down and across about role size, functions, and process accountabilities).

During the role and process interviews, a collection of problems, opportunities, and critical issues is compiled. Obviously, the more experienced the practitioner or consultant supporting the organization's OD project teams is, the more accurate and useful these preliminary findings will be.

Next, the senior executive group works to confirm and refine the emerging picture of the actual organization and clarify how it does and does not support the accountable, capable, and efficient execution of strategy. This iterative process helps the executive team to further modify its strategic view. In particular, the process helps them to examine the best logic for defining its businesses and markets. This begins the phase of modeling alternative structures and, ultimately, deciding on the *ideal* structure to support the newly defined strategy.

LEAD: From Structure to People

During the structural modeling phase, an assessment of the potential and effectiveness of the top 100 to 200 managers is conducted. The capabilities identified in the senior-management pool need to be reconciled with the requirements of the ideal structure to determine whether there is a good match. The information gained here, together with the capabilities of the existing processes and infrastructure to support the ideal structure, will determine whether transitional structures must be built to get from the *actual* organization to the *ideal* organization.

Once the intermediate or transitional structure is decided upon, role-filling activities can be undertaken confidently using the assessments of potential and effectiveness that I outlined in Chapter 6 and Chapter 10. After deciding who needs to go where, the transition requirements of reassigning, transferring, and cross-training can be finalized and a transition plan more fully developed.

Again, I cannot stress enough how critical it is to have a well-orchestrated communication plan to fully explicate the changes throughout the various implementation phases.

LEAD: From People to Processes and Systems

Any structure will support function only as well as the managers and subordinates working within it effectively apply the LEAD principles. It is critical to provide effective, practical training and facilitation of the managerial, teamworking, and process-leadership practices described throughout this book. This also requires knowledgeable practitioners to bring the merits of the new ways of working to life.

With a cadre of knowledgeable managers in newly defined roles, the next phase of clarifying the details of process accountabilities begins. This facilitated undertaking helps to ensure accountable, capable, and efficient processes and systems. This phase helps to more fully define the accountabilities of each role in relation to each process. It also establishes accountabilities for system stewardship.

LEAD: From Systems Back to Strategy

We have now come full circle. Along with other HR systems not covered in this book, the final phase of implementation ensures the ongoing renewal of engagement, alignment, and development systems. In particular, the talent pool–development system is critical for ensuring the effective recruitment, assessment, development, selection, compensation, and retention of top talent. It is through the ongoing application of effective leadership and what I call "people stewardship" that the full potential of the organization will be fully realized.

Coupled with strong system stewardship based on strategic LEAD principles, accountability leadership becomes ingrained in the organization's DNA.

---

[1]Harry Levinson (with Charlton R. Price, Kenneth J. Munden, Harold J. Mandl, and Charles M. Solley), *Men, Management, and Mental Health,* p. 22.
[2]Harry Levinson, *Ready, Fire, Aim: Avoiding Management by Impulse,* p. 130.

Part IV:
Applications and Afterthoughts

Merely understanding—much less installing—a genuine LEAD system can be a daunting undertaking. The goal of *Accountability Leadership* is to provide you with a level of awareness that will enable you to embark on this profitable adventure.

In Part I we looked at the role of accountability in organizations. In Part II we examined the four elements of the LEAD system: leverage, engagement, alignment, and development. In Part III you learned how to create accountability in teams, processes, and whole leadership systems.

In this final section we walk a few steps further and investigate LEAD from other perspectives. In this way, your comprehension of accountability leadership will deepen, arming you with greater confidence and knowledge as you lead the charge in your company toward this brave new world.

Chapter 12

Taking LEAD on the Road

How does the LEAD process stack up against other managerial systems and approaches? When you look around, you can find variations and pieces of LEAD principles that in some cases are effective and in others suffer from their lack of integration with full LEAD implementation. Here are three articles and one book review published in the business trade press in recent years that caught my eye. My analysis (which follows each) provides greater understanding of the implications and effectiveness of LEAD.

(**Note:** Each selection is reprinted in full by written permission of its copyright holder.)

How Quint Studer Used Quarterly Evaluations to Help Baptist Hospital Reach its Goal of Becoming the Employer of Choice

Source: *Inc.* (Interview)
Issue: March, 1999
© 1999 Goldhirsh Group, Inc.

It's a cliche these days to say that the best way to satisfy your customers is to satisfy your employees. Like favoring motherhood and apple pie, it's a hard thesis to argue against. But as a manager, how do you get started?

How do you actually change a company's culture? And how do you know if you're succeeding? Until we met up with Quinton Studer, president of Baptist Hospital Inc., in Pensacola, Fla., we were skeptical of those advocating cultural change within an organization. Most had never given it a try in the real world.

Studer, who arrived in Pensacola in June 1996 from a stint as senior vice-president at Holy Cross Hospital in Chicago, has spent the last several years developing a system to improve both patient and employee satisfaction. Surprisingly, the model is based on his years as a special-education teacher.

"Maximizing an organization's ability is similar to maximizing a child's potential," Studer says. "The first step is to diagnose the situation and then set achievable goals. The higher the goals, the closer the student—or organization—comes to reaching full potential.

"Every 90 days the teacher does an individual education plan to ensure that all resources directed to the child are aligned with the goals. And at the end of a year, old goals are reassessed and new ones are set."

While that's the basic plan, Studer has refined his system over the years and brought it to the point where it's replicable not only in other hospitals but in any service business. When Studer arrived, Baptist's admissions were flat, and patient satisfaction as measured by a national survey was slightly below average. After just two years—in an industry in which admissions are staying the same or going down—Baptist's admissions were up 8.3%. Outpatient volume was up 33%. As for patient satisfaction, Baptist ranked number two in the country for all hospitals and number one for hospitals with more than 100 beds. Employee satisfaction had improved 30%, and physician satisfaction had risen from 72.4% to 81.3%. Job turnover for nurses went from 30% to 18%. Inc. senior editor Nancy J. Lyons queried Studer about Baptist's cultural turnaround.

Inc.: Changing a culture seems more than ambitious—it's an absolutely daunting idea. Yet you seem to have accomplished a great deal in a very short time at Baptist. How did you get started?

Studer: We decided we had to have a measurable service goal. I believe you have to measure what's important to you, and that you have to have some means of comparison. If a company can't afford an outside group to do a survey, which I strongly recommend, it should develop its own tool. So, first of all, we met with all the employees and talked about why the hospital exists, what our purpose is. They said that they wanted to be the best. Becoming the employer of choice also became a goal at Baptist.

Inc.: So you started out measuring patient satisfaction?

Studer: Yes. We use a large patient-satisfaction-measurement company that can compare us with at least 500 hospitals across the country. We send a survey to every patient. The results help us set specific goals. They also give us an opportunity to recognize employees who receive positive comments on the survey.

Inc.: Okay, so you know where you stand from the survey, and you know where you want to go. But up to now, nothing has changed, right? It seems that this would be where most CEOs would get stuck.

Studer: What we do next is the number one thing companies just don't want to spend money on: middle-management development. We take every one of our leaders—nurse managers, supervisors, and department heads—off-site for 2 days every 90 days. We also have employee forums every 90 days and survey employees on their attitudes toward their supervisors. Our employees knew their supervisors hadn't had any "real" training, but we also let them know it's an organizational issue—not their supervisor's issue—to provide development. We call it leadership muscle building. That's what my whole job is about. Accountability, by the way, is key.

Inc.: What do you mean by accountability? Who's accountable to whom and for what?

Studer: All our leaders get "report cards" every 90 days. That's how we align behaviors to our goals and how we can reward objectively, which takes politics out of the game. A typical person in our organization will have four measurements. One is customer service, which we measure against our goal, which is to be in the top 1% of hospitals in the country. All the employees know what will satisfy our customers and where our weaknesses lie, because they know the results of the patient-satisfaction survey. The second measurement looks at efficiency: how long patients are in their units per diagnosis. The third one is expense management: how well they're managing expenses. The fourth thing we're measuring this year is turnover. Everyone's got a turnover goal based on his or her unit and its past history.

Inc.: When you say everyone has a turn-over goal, does that include top managers as well?

Studer: Yes, our vice-presidents also have their own report cards and are measured on the same four categories as middle managers are. Twenty percent of my incentive compensation is based on employee turnover. That gets my attention.

Inc.: What sorts of things do you do to slow down the turnover?

Studer: We used the same sort of survey tool to measure employee satisfaction as we'd used to measure customer satisfaction. We found out that the biggest thing that bugged our employees was that their evaluations were late. They want feedback. Employees also want supervisors who accept their input with respect and appreciation. They want to know about matters that affect them. So we measured. And we set goals for where we wanted to be. We took all our leaders off-site and taught them how to present the survey data. Then we did 90-day work plans with employees, itemizing what we were going to change in the workplace to make it better. Then we measured again, and rewarded and recognized our accomplishments. I believe in strong rewards and recognition.

Inc.: What sort of rewards and recognition?

Studer: Every company has outstanding people. We make heroes of them. One of our nurses, Cyd Cadena, called up a lady who had been hospitalized to see how she was doing at home. She was in a wheelchair, and she was depressed because she didn't have a wheelchair ramp. The family was so busy working on home health care and a whole bunch of other things that they didn't get a chance to put in a ramp. Well, Cyd called our plant-management person, Don Swartz. And guess what Don did? He built a ramp. Don didn't ask, "Can I do it?" I found out about it because the patient called me. Now we tell that story all over the whole organization. What did we tell our people it was OK to do? Break a few rules. Take a few risks. Don is a star. You have to celebrate your legends.

***Inc.*:** Tell us some of the other things that Baptist Hospital is doing to make it "the employer of choice."

Studer: Anybody who's ever been in a hospital knows we lose stuff. Patients complain about lost glasses, lost dentures, lost robes. And we ask dumb questions like "Are you sure you brought them with you?" "Are you sure your family doesn't have them?" "Why don't we wait and maybe they'll show up after discharge?" That leaves the employee dealing with a very unhappy patient, who doesn't get a check from us until three weeks after he or she has left the hospital. Today we have $250 available for any employee in the hospital to access on the spot to cover the cost of a patient's lost glasses or whatever

We had a crazy rule in housekeeping that bugged the employees. Only our housekeepers were allowed to have housekeeping supplies. So if a nurse on a unit spilled something, and the unit coordinator or nurse wanted to clean it up, he or she couldn't. Instead, people spent 20 minutes saying, "Watch out! Don't step there. We've called housekeeping." Why weren't we allowing our staff to have housekeeping supplies in their unit? Trust. They might have taken them home. We didn't know we were this crazy until we started asking the employees what they needed.

***Inc.*:** Any other advice for CEOs on getting employees to buy into their ideas for change?

Studer: Well, you have to really believe in what you're doing. When I got to Baptist, I said, "We're going to be the best hospital in the country," and somebody said, "Quint, you mean county." I said, "No, I mean country." You have to decide what you want to do, act on that decision, and look at the results. Then you get understanding. Sometimes we just have to get people to change their behavior and then they'll understand what we're after.

I'll give you an example. We have a rule at Baptist: We don't point. We think it's rude. We take people to where they're going. The other day I got a nice letter from a patient who said what impressed him the most was that when he walked into the hospital, somebody took him to where he needed to go. I don't know who it was, but whoever it was was a caregiver at that moment. Now, Bob Harriman, the VP of ambulatory care—he told me this later—thought it was a dumb idea. He didn't have time to guide people through the hospital. But I had to believe that if you actually take patients to where they need to go, it'll make a difference in how they view the hospital. We made the decision that's what we were going to do, and basically forced it for a while. The second time Harriman took someone to where that person was going, he understood and became a believer.

So sometimes we've just got to get people to do the behavior and then trust that they'll understand it afterward and become believers. You can get so hung up on getting everybody to understand what you're doing and why you're doing it that it never happens. Don't overworry about understanding. It will come, provided you act.

Analysis

Quint Studer appears to follow many of the LEAD principles and practices. He recognizes the importance of leveraging every employee's potential to deliver on ambitious, value-adding goals and to develop every manager into an effective leader.

The article doesn't describe the communication practices taught to, and expected from, his managers, so it is difficult to comment on them. Employee expectations of managers are listed and do imply the type of engagement and alignment practices covered in LEAD. The clear definition of goals (QQTRs), measurement of their outcomes, and reward/recognition for success parallels closely our alignment leadership practices. Studer's strong insistence on aligning authority with accountability resonates very closely with LEAD principles.

The article is not clear on whether the appraisals, leading to reward and recognition, are tied to individual (vs. group) performance and whether the targets are a given, so that it is employee effectiveness that is really appraised. If compensation were tied only to measurable outputs, this would be at odds with LEAD, because much of employee value cannot be directly measured, even though it can be accurately appraised.

Studer's opening comparison with special education is interesting and informative. He clearly believes that individuals and organizations typically function well below their potential. (I strongly agree.) He also believes that one must set high standards and specific goals to help people tap into that unused potential. Studer understands that people need meaningful work if they are to be strongly motivated and he helps to forge that meaning by seeking and using employee input directly and indirectly.

Studer is also clear about tying employee targets and actions to the bigger picture. But it is not clear to me whether he expects each manager, at every level, to set specific context to ensure the most accurate understanding by each employee of her specific piece of that larger puzzle.

The strong emphasis on development is key. No one can expect individuals to be effective in complex roles unless they are given them the necessary tools, training, information, and feedback.

Leadership Skills Employees Respect: Communication, Accountability, and Trust are What Employers Need from Executives

Source: *Nation's Business*
Author: Michael Barrier
Issue: January 1999
© 1999 U.S. Chamber of Commerce

The critical areas are communication, accountability, and trust. You might think that being the CEO of a small business automatically qualifies you as its leader. But Pamela Barefoot, president of Blue Crab Bay Co., a producer of specialty foods and gifts in Onancock, Va., says: "I felt like I was in the back seat of the car and nobody was driving. My lack of confidence in where we were going and how we were going to get there affected everybody."

Barefoot started Blue Crab Bay in her home in 1985, selling gift baskets of Virginia products. Sales rose from $5,000 in her first year to $600,000 five years later, but this financial success aggravated rather than eased Barefoot's anxiety.

"I was scared because I didn't know what I was doing," she says. "I'd never run a company before. This company was growing so fast, and we were undercapitalized, and everything I had was on the line. I had to decide: Am I going to get on this horse and ride it, or am I just going to stand on the sidelines and let it run ahead?"

With the help of a consulting firm, Barefoot did find a way to get onto that horse. Now Blue Crab and its two dozen employees are about to move into a 12,500-square-foot building in an industrial park in Melfa, Va.

Like other successful small-business people, Barefoot developed crucial leadership skills in three areas that can be summed up under the headings communication, accountability, and trust. Think of them, if you will, as the big CAT.

The advice of experts and the testimony of business people suggests that if you can develop CAT skills, there's a good chance you'll become ruler of the jungle.

Communication

In writings on leadership and in business people's accounts of their own leadership crises, the ability to communicate effectively emerges repeatedly as the most important skill to cultivate.

In Barefoot's case, the first move toward developing this skill was writing a mission statement that would clarify for her employees—and for Barefoot herself—what the firm was all about. A mission statement lays out a company's goals and articulates the principles that the company will adhere to as it tries to reach those goals.

A small-business owner with a clear sense of purpose may regard a mission statement as superfluous. "It can often feel almost corny to write out something that everybody [in the company] already knows," explains Michael Useem, director of the Center for Leadership and Change at the University of Pennsylvania's Wharton School.

But, he says, "in any setting, you need to be clear about your vision and very articulate in getting it across to people you want to go with you. You need to have a very strong team built up before you really need to use it to its maximum.["]

A mission statement is still only a first step, however. You also need what Useem, author of *The Leadership Moment* (Times Business, $25), calls "routine communication to remind everybody" of what "the point is of working so hard. You can't tell people too often where you're going, what the vision is."

Barefoot believes that you should start devoting attention to communication when your company grows to more than five or six employees. "It seems as if every time we get upset here, or something goes wrong," she says, "it's because we're not communicating. Somebody will say something, and somebody else will hear it a different way."

What consultant and author Patrick Lencioni calls "the need to structure a lot of things that have been occurring in the company naturally" arises as a company grows larger and informal communication based on day-to-day contact becomes more difficult. "What they want most is growth," Lencioni says of the leaders of such businesses, "and yet when growth occurs, they resist doing the things they need to do to continue to fuel that growth."

When a start-up company has perhaps 10 employees, Useem says, "it's very personal, with typically very strong loyalty between you and the people who come in. By the time you get up to a couple of hundred, your ability to exercise authority, or to get people to work real hard, no longer can rely on that personal daily contact. You've got to lead through other means. Your words begin to count a lot more."

When you say something to 300 people, he adds, "it has staying power way beyond a similar statement when you've got three." People are seeing you less and hearing you less, and for that reason what you say when they do see and hear you counts for more. Your way of communicating must change as you grow, but what about the content of that communication? Whatever the size of the firm, you should share information with your employees "that allows them to feel that they've achieved a certain set of objectives," says New York City-based consultant Gary Brooks, chairman of the Institute of Management Consultants.

"If you divorce the employees from that sense of accomplishment," he says, "they really don't know what they're there for and what to strive for. The more that you can involve them in the creation of the targets, and then keep them posted as to how they've progressed against those targets, the happier the employees. Most people need objectives to work toward."

A small business's leader must constantly reinforce and explain those objectives. That is the lesson suggested by the experience of Bob Tingey, president and chief operating officer of Sorenco Laboratories, a privately held, 55-employee company in Salt Lake City that manufactures private-label personal-care products.

After he became president of Sorenco six years ago, Tingey began changing the company's manufacturing processes to bring them into line with the ideas of the quality-management movement. "At the very beginning," he says, "it was like dragging a dead horse. I was tempted many times to say, 'If you can't do it this way, you need to find somewhere else to work.'"

Instead, Tingey took the trouble, repeatedly, to explain the reasons for the changes and to show their advantages. "When we would catch a problem that we would have missed" under the old system, he says, "I would bring people together and have a little teaching moment," explaining how the change had saved the company money. As he did, resistance gradually melted.

Accountability

If you're successful in communicating your company's goals to your employees, you're only partway home; you must hold them accountable for how well they perform in striving toward those goals.

"A lot of CEOs in small companies create a family-like atmosphere in the company, which is great," says Lencioni, author of *The Five Temptations of a CEO* (Jossey-Bass, $20). "But that makes it difficult for them to separate popularity from accountability." It's by holding employees accountable, he says, that you earn their respect.

You can't hold people accountable for reaching goals, though, Brooks says, unless you've given them "the authority to achieve those goals." Neither does holding people accountable mean abusing them. As Brooks says, "Nobody likes to get yelled and screamed at."

There's no yelling and screaming when something goes wrong at Accommodations by Apple, a 14-employee company in Lenexa, Kan., that specializes in corporate relocations to the Kansas City area. Founder Kierstin Higgins says that when, say, a client explodes in anger over a perceived shortcoming in the firm's services, "we try to round-table everybody together" and discuss what happened to understand why the client reacted that way.

Because the services are so personal—ranging from airport pickups to the transfer of medical records, with an emphasis on family matters—and the demands accordingly severe, "it's important to shore [the employees] up," Higgins says. "Our employees are very young and energetic, but they're also very emotional, with major ups and major downs."

"Trying to help them learn from the challenges they've experienced, as opposed to getting burned out," is, she believes, the essence of being a good leader in her company.

Likewise, Tingey says, "whenever something goes wrong around here, we never go after the person who messed up. The question we ask is what process doesn't exist, or what process let us down and needs to be improved?"

That doesn't mean bad apples won't turn up or that they shouldn't be tossed out, he says. "But if people are following the process and something goes wrong, there's never a word said to the people involved"—because, he says, "it's almost always because management hasn't prepared the process well enough, or trained them well enough."

In other words, you have to hold yourself accountable, too, and do so with increasing self-awareness as your company grows beyond your ability to control the details of its operation.

Lencioni says decisiveness is an area where small-company owners must measure themselves rigorously. Being decisive usually isn't a problem for the owner of a very small company who has to make quick decisions if the firm is to survive. But it may become a problem as the company grows and its survival seems assured. Another critical measure of your own performance, the experts suggest, is how willing you are to give other people some of the authority you have been exercising. "If you're micromanaging," Useem says, "you're definitely not leading."

By the time you get up to several hundred employees, he says, the caliber of your management team has become extremely important, "because at that scale, you just can't get things to happen yourself. You need a cadre of people who are leaders in their own right."

At Blue Crab Bay, Barefoot has already created new layers of management—not to separate herself from her employees, but to entrust authority to supervisors. She had to delegate more, she says, "so I could concentrate on what I was good at," such as expanding the company's product lines.

Trust

You've communicated clearly and constantly to your employees what your company is about. You've held yourself as well as your employees accountable for how well they're going about achieving the company's goals. The fruit of such a shared effort should be a deepening trust that can free both business owner and employees to do their best.

"You have to trust them to be making good decisions," Useem says. "They have to trust you to know where you're going. There's no rocket science involved. Trust is engendered through openness, integrity, clarity of expression—it's the accumulated product of saying what you're going to do, and doing it, and getting results."

Says Barefoot of her employees: "They know how I feel about things, and when I leave here they can run this business just as well as I can, because they know the way I want it done." She now takes extended foreign trips that she would have found unthinkable a few years ago.

Among other things, a sense of shared purpose can free an owner from the need to deal with a problem employee. "Things get resolved a lot faster now" in such cases, Barefoot says, because her managers and employees "have the confidence to step in there and get it straight."

Trust can also strengthen your company when a crisis occurs. Accommodations by Apple lost one of its largest clients in a downsizing in 1997. Higgins laid out the situation to her employees, even though she feared they might leave when they knew how dire the situation was. "They all stayed," she says, adding that she and her employees sought out new accounts, "and we built up enough revenue to keep all of those employees."

Trust is a personal thing, though. What happens when your company has grown to 30 or 40 employees and it has employees that you didn't even interview or that you don't see very often?

"The key is to focus on maintaining that trust among your direct reports," Lencior says. "As the company grows, the CEO has to accept a more limited span of direct control and really work to ensure that direct span is stronger than ever before."

The rewards of being an effective leader can be measured not just in the steady growth of companies such as Blue Crab Bay and Sorenco Laboratories and in the survival of companies such as Accommodations by Apple but also in the psychic satisfaction felt by the leaders themselves.

"I'm braver in a lot of areas," Barefoot says. "In 1990, I didn't even know how to turn on a computer. I didn't know how to read a financial statement, and I'm not intimidated by that anymore."

Says Sorenco Laboratories' Tingey: "The first three years I was here, I didn't sleep very well, worrying about everything—worrying about whether what was on that pallet was what the customer wanted, worrying about whether people were going to show up to do the job. I sleep well now."

Analysis

This article illustrates that there is no single formula (LEAD vs. CAT) for informing managers how to become effective leaders. However, the article strongly points out that leadership is about leverage, consistent with LEAD.

And good communication is inherent in engagement, alignment, and development:

- Engagement requires all of those communication attributes (open, honest, direct disclosure) necessary to build a strong, reciprocal, and trust-inducing psychological contract.
- Alignment depends on the types of communications necessary for setting clear context and defining precise QQTRs.
- Development also requires ongoing, accurate, behaviorally anchored communication about feedback (employee effectiveness), gap analyses (opportunities to work closer to potential), and career analyses (steps necessary to work at potential throughout one's career).

However, accountability is given short shrift in this piece. It does not imply, as the *Inc.* article about Quint Studer does, that accountability is only about outputs. This article does make the point that accountability is the basis of mature working relationships and is, therefore, healthy.

There are several points where the author emphasizes the importance of aligning accountability with authority. The point is also made that people are more committed to their targets when they have input into defining them. Finally, important emphasis is placed on the relationship between being able to meet accountabilities and deliver results and the integrity of the processes supporting them.

As with communication, trust is inherent in all aspects of LEAD. There are two ways to engage employees with their company: coercion (fear, manipulation, exploitation, extortion, and so on) and cohesion. The basis of cohesion is a healthy psychological contract in which the organization harnesses the intrinsic, positive motivation of its employees. It requires a sense of common purpose, proper distance (characterized by mutual trust and reciprocity), and mutual support during change. The bottom line is that employees must be able to trust their managers.

No Piece of Cake: Whether You're a Pastry Chef or the President, Ethical Leadership Has to Start at the Top

Source: *Nation's* Restaurant News
Issue: October 2, 2000
© 2000 Lebhar-Friedman, Inc.

Franette McColloch is the latest in a long list of women to be linked to President Clinton in a sexual context, but not in the way Gennifer Flowers or Monica Lewinsky were linked to him. A White House pastry chef since 1983, McColloch allegedly endured sexual overtures from her boss, head pastry chef Roland Mesnier, for the past nine years.

She recently filed a lawsuit against Mesnier, accusing him of, among other things, having asked her to touch him inappropriately, making harassing phone calls and, finally, retaliating against her repeated rejections with overly burdensome assignments, such as peeling a huge volume of kiwi fruit for a state dinner.

The lawsuit also claims that the supervisor who oversaw the kitchen failed to address McColloch's repeated complaints, and it names President Clinton as a defendant for failing to have in place within the White House a system for addressing sexual harassment problems.

Although some White House officials declined to comment on the pending litigation, spokesman Joe Lockhart disputed McColloch's contention that employees had no recourse when they believed they had been discriminated against. "Everyone here at the White House is committed to ensuring equal employment opportunity for all employees, and we take any suggestion or allegation of discrimination seriously," Lockhart said during a press briefing.

He noted that employee grievances may be filed with the White House Equal Employment Opportunity Office, where they are handled in accordance with federal antidiscrimination law, which requires counseling and mediation before a case proceeds to the courts. He also noted that employees receive a 15-page manual explaining their rights under the law and the procedures available to protect them. Mesnier's employment status has not changed since the suit was filed.

While it is unlikely that Clinton's past philandering provided any role models for the alleged harasser in McColloch's case, the fact remains that the chief executive of any organization should bear ultimate responsibility when employees feel they are constrained in reporting harassment or discrimination. Federal statutes say as much, hence Bill Clinton's ironic involvement as a defendant in a case where, for a change, he is not the alleged aggressor. And the same kind of accountability ought to extend to the leaders of foodservice firms.

Of course, the truth of McColloch's allegations should be determined in a court of law, where the accused can present a defense. Still, one can only hope that this was not a case of a leader who engaged in unsavory conduct and influenced the behavior of a subordinate. If the official message in the White House is "Do as I say, not as I do," was the perceived message, "I don't really care"?

President Clinton made headlines with his transgressions even before he moved into the Oval Office. He publicly apologized for his long affair with Flowers, and he publicly lamented his trysts with White House intern Lewinsky. He even has been the direct subject of a sexual-harassment charge himself, denying for years the complaint lodged against him by Arkansas state employee Paula Jones.

Of course, that denial does not excuse the inappropriate behavior of someone who works for him, if in fact that occurred. But it could make it hard for Clinton, under any circumstances, to enforce protocols that he himself appears to ignore.

"I am a long-term, dedicated White House employee, who just wanted to do my job," McColloch said in a statement. "I was shocked when White House officials told me that they would not interfere with my supervisor's 'management style' to stop the sexual harassment and encouraged me to leave if I did not like the situation." The legal system must now weigh the details.

Given the testosterone-laced pall that has so often tainted the Clinton administration, McColloch's case comes as a disturbing reminder of things that many Americans might prefer to forget. If she has fabricated the entire incident, then her attorneys know a doubt-ridden and potentially lucrative situation when they see one. And if she didn't, her grievance would be a powerful reminder that all administrations, whether in government or the private sector, must protect vulnerable employees from unsavory aggressors.

Because the heated atmospheres of kitchens have been catalysts in numerous instances of sexual discrimination, foodservice managers in particular must keep that fact in mind when they lay down the rules.

Analysis

This article gets to the core of accountability leadership. In particular, it provokes thought about the difference between accountable *for* and accountable *to.*

The nature of managerial hierarchies is that all managers are accountable for their subordinates' outputs, their subordinates' effectiveness in role, and ensuring that their subordinates operate within defined limits. This fundamental law of organizational gravity clearly applies to this article. President Clinton was accountable for ensuring that a system is in place (policies and effective managers supporting those policies) that should identify unacceptable behaviors in employees and require their managers to hold them accountable (or be held accountable themselves).

There is no wiggle room around this in the basic principles of accountability leadership. Remember that a chain is only as strong as its weakest link. In an employment (managerial leadership) system—as opposed to elected political system—this point is clearly enforceable. The shareholders must hold the board accountable for ensuring the CEO meets these requirements. The board can remove the CEO if he doesn't. The shareholders can remove the board if it fails to act. It is by its very nature an accountability hierarchy.

The source of authority and accountability is different, however, in a political system. The president of the United States has no board of directors with such authority to hold him accountable. Hence, the role of Congress in impeaching a president replaces this mechanism. Yet the standards for impeachment are more stringent. Of course, the electorate can choose not to reelect the president, but that also is a less direct form of "being called to account."

The second point about the moral and ethical standard set by a CEO is less directly covered by LEAD, but it is certainly implied in engagement and the psychological contract. Positional authority by itself is insufficient to fully engage employees. (Remember coercion vs. cohesion?) Managerial leaders must *earn* the respect and enthusiastic commitment of their people to fully apply themselves, within the requirements of the accountability framework. When managers demonstrate a personal disregard for the letter or the spirit of a policy, they lose personal credibility and they confer a similar disrespect onto their people for that policy.

Managers (beginning with shareholders and boards) must articulate what is inside and what is outside their value systems. Then they must define the minimal standards of behavior expected to support those values. The higher the managerial position, the stronger the message its occupant gives to the organization when adhering to—or deviating from—those standards and values in his own behavior. This is yet another example of leadership as leverage.

The Quest for Responsibility:
Accountability and Citizenship in Complex Organizations

Source: Cornell University Review
Author: Marcia P. Miceli
Issue: December 1999
© 1999 Cornell University, Johnson Graduate School
Book publication information: Mark Bovens, author.
Cambridge University Press, 1998.

In *The Quest for Responsibility,* Bovens has undertaken the difficult task of determining how top managers and other organization members can be made appropriately responsible for fraud, pollution, and other wrongdoing that occurs in organizations. Obviously, such a complex question requires an interdisciplinary approach. Drawing from law, organization theory, organizational behavior, ethics, philosophy, sociology, public policy and management, and other areas of inquiry, Bovens takes great care in analyzing the question. As professor of legal philosophy at the University of Utrecht and a policy advisor to the Ministry of Justice of the Netherlands, he emphasizes analysis of the issues over the development of organization theory and exhaustive review of empirical research. Yet he does an admirable job of integrating work from areas outside his own. He does not package a set of prescriptions for managers, though a chapter devoted to practical implications is included. Readers comfortable with the emphases Professor Bovens has chosen will likely find the book challenging and interesting.

Bovens essentially proposes that it is hard to understand how serious wrongdoing in organizations can occur and recur. Aside from the ethical reasons not to engage in it, it seems reasonable to propose that rational decision makers would see that the negative consequences of allowing wrongdoing to continue would usually outweigh any short-run benefit to the organization. The consequences can be disastrous not only for victims, but for the organizations themselves, well beyond the costs of fines or other immediate financial losses. For example, many consumers' views of Ford are still colored by the Pinto fiasco, and the lives of members of financial institutions can be greatly affected by the imposition of complex and costly regulations. Further, most public accounts of organizational wrongdoing mention that persons within the organization recognized that serious problems were brewing. But they didn't act, or their warnings to others were simply ignored.

Why?

Bovens proposes that the answer lies in the "problem of many hands"— that in complex organizations it is difficult to attribute responsibility to the organization as a whole and that where attributions to individuals are made, impediments to accepting full responsibility abound. This position seems reminiscent of two theoretical streams that are not discussed in the book. First, research on the diffusion of responsibility and bystander intervention (e.g., Latane and Darley, 1968) proposes that the greater the number of observers of wrongdoing such as street crime, the less likely that any of them will feel morally responsible for acting. Second, agency theory (Fama and Jensen, 1983; Eisenhardt, 1989) suggests that organizations must align incentives for their agents (employees) to act in ways that are congruent with organizational goals.

The author does not claim to have the solutions. He describes models of "passive" responsibility and "active" responsibility and critiques each, though he favors one of the individual models. Bovens offers some interesting suggestions that could be viewed as empirical questions. For example, his analysis suggests that, except at the highest levels of management, training people to behave more "morally" will fail without the appropriate structure for supporting and enforcing such behavior. He suggests that the problems are exacerbated by organizational size but does not recommend breaking large organizations into smaller units.

The international perspectives taken were quite interesting. I was struck by how often the author noted similar findings or legal outcomes across multiple cultures and legal systems. Of course, much of the work concerned British, Australian, U.S., and Western European systems, and many extensions remain to be considered. Overall, *The Quest for Responsibility* is thought provoking and demands careful reading. It may well serve as a springboard for organization theorists to develop research propositions.

Analysis

The author provides a provocative sociological perspective that accurately describes many pieces of the puzzle. However, he ultimately fails to identify the key to its solution. His book implies that managerial or employment hierarchies are mere replications of natural social units or social democracies. This is simply not true.

The book also hints at the solution when it calls on the need for the "appropriate structure for supporting and enforcing such behavior." Yet, it fails to clarify that managerial systems are, by their very nature, accountability hierarchies. Remember that managers are accountable for ensuring that all employees in their subordinate organization work within prescribed limits (policies, procedures, rules, regulations, and so forth). If a manager fails to define, monitor, and maintain these limits by calling subordinate "outliers" to account, then that manager should himself be called to account.

This process begins with the shareholders and the board, who are accountable for establishing a charter and operating the company within legal requirements. The board, in turn, has a fiduciary accountability to establish auditing systems and to monitor compliance within them by the CEO and the employment organization. The CEO, in turn, must lead globally with appropriate systems and systems stewardship. The CEO must also manage locally by holding each subordinate manager accountable for the compliance of his subordinate employees with the requirements of those systems.

In a managerial hierarchy, the prevention of wrongdoing is straightforward and uncomplicated. Define the rules. Ensure that people understand the rules. Design processes that comply with the rules. Educate people how to operate those processes within the rules. Observe whether they adhere to the rules, and hold them accountable when they do not.

The "problem of many hands" occurs when organizations and their leaders fail to get clear definition about "who is accountable for what in relation to whom and within what limits." This is not an inevitable consequence of having large, complex organizations. Rather, it is a consequence of applying inadequate knowledge and what I call managerial abdication. The solution? Accountability leadership, of course!

Chapter 13
From the Annals of Consultation

When clients of The Levinson Institute discover the power of LEAD, they find themselves moving forward to more productive ways of doing business. In this chapter, we look at three case studies from our files that demonstrate clearly—and remarkably—how accountability leadership works. To maintain client confidentiality, the identities of these companies and managers have been altered.

Case #1: Northern Pine

One company I have seen profit by accountability leadership principles is a producer of forest products, pulp, and newsprint called Northern Pine (NP), located in Washington State. Northern Pine had been watching its productivity levels drop steadily for over five years, but rather than sell the company off, management had decided to attempt to turn the situation around.

Embarking on a full-scale organizational diagnosis of NP's managerial structure as well as its managerial practices, I uncovered these four critical issues:

1. There were too many managerial layers, resulting in too many levels of approval and role compression with the lack of managerial value added.

2. There were confused accountabilities with many line managers trying to perform their duties without the requisite authorities.

3. NP managers employed no system-wide use of context setting. This resulted in most employees feeling as though they were doing piecework and otherwise "flying blind."

4. Many employees found themselves in roles that they were not optimally suited for. There was a company-wide mismatch of horsepower, skilled knowledge, and commitment. In other words, the right people were in the wrong roles.

Following my diagnosis and a thorough review of NP's managerial system from an accountability leadership perspective, leaders implemented the following changes:

1. After a six-month period of reorganization, top management established the optimal number of managerial levels across all three divisions of the company.

2. Top management more carefully fit individuals into specific roles. At the same time, coaching and mentoring led to more active and accurate development of people.

3. Managers instituted context setting as well iterative two-way dialogue resulting in aligned, ambitious, and achievable assignments. No longer did managers just bark out orders to their subordinates.

4. Top management instituted unambiguous lines of accountability between managers, subordinates, and cross-functional peers working together on cross-functional processes.

Within a year, as accountabilities for continuous improvement became clear, employees and managers began to show more enthusiasm and personal initiative. In general, morale and teamwork began to flourish at NP.

In terms of metrics, NP's output rose 35 percent despite a 20-percent reduction in personnel. The company quickly moved to the top of its industry in areas such as product quality and product delivery. Not surprisingly, customer satisfaction ratings rose dramatically across the board. Aggregate customer rejects in all three divisions, for example, fell by 50 percent. These figures compared favorably to industry benchmarks, something NP had not achieved in quite a long time.

Case #2: Gulf State Power

Very committed for years to extensive use of "quality" teams, Gulf State Power (GSP) abruptly switched gears in June 1990. To the surprise of company insiders and outsiders alike, GSP's new chairman announced that quality teams and similar empowerment programs at GSP were to be henceforth discontinued. Instead, the company planned to revisit an old, discredited (to industry watchers) idea: holding employees accountable individually for the quality of the work they did every day.

Reporting on the news, a leading business magazine explained that GSP's workforce—employees, line managers, middle and upper management—had for some time been complaining of a loss of individual initiative and responsibility. The most common cause cited was a kind of parallel group-based quality bureaucracy. Two hierarchies were operating at once: a managerial hierarchy and a quality one. Each was competing with the other. The quality hierarchy steadily grew into the group-based bureaucracy. Everyone felt swallowed up by the many groups they found themselves reporting to.

GSP employees also said they no longer felt any connection to the results of their work. They felt as though they carried out their assignments in a vacuum, never seeing directly the impact of whatever they did. Employees also reported their level of authority in any given assignment was usually unclear.

In terms of accountability leadership, GSP's managers had completely lost sight of the proper balance between accountability and authority. Line managers had begun holding employees accountable for quantity while quality managers held them accountable for quality. Their sense of outputs and processes seemed totally unconnected to each other, obscuring the company's overriding mission. People had separate process (quality) missions and results-based (quantity) missions, and never the twain shall meet!

Fortunately, upper management finally recognized the problem and took the reins back, sending the organization in an accountability direction. Within the next few years, the company shifted toward rekindled morale and a renewed focus on growth.

Case #3: Titanium Enterprises

This example was briefly alluded to in Chapter 1. I offer it in more detail here for a fuller understanding of the difference between responsibility and accountability.

Despite some success at doing his job, and in some ways more success than anyone else ever had doing it, top management at Titanium Enterprises felt that one of their managers, Sam Travers, needed to drastically change his ways. Sam had been employed by the company for more than 12 years and had been a good employee for all of that time. Since his promotion to assistant superintendent, though, he had grown increasingly grouchy, disruptive, dysfunctional, and outright mean.

Name a complaint and Titanium management probably fielded one just like it from machine operators about Sam. Sam was accountable for keeping fabrication machines running at high levels of productivity. His management style was to yell, threaten, curse, and even throw loud tantrums, kicking cans around at times, always getting very upset. Curiously, this behavior only began after Sam had been promoted to his present position, a move the company considered a reward to him for his years of good service. Before this, he had never been known to act this way.

But why would such a move cause such a 180-degree behavior shift? Shouldn't Sam's promotion have made him happier, content, confident, and respectful? For whatever reason, it obviously had not.

To keep reaching for higher levels of production, so urgent in an industry plagued by fierce global competition, Titanium's top managers had felt that the company needed more capable processes as well as more capable employees to support them. Titanium employees were being asked to do ambitious things, to meet quotas and volume goals heretofore unimagined. It was a challenging company to work for, its executives boasted. The key to making it all work was a combination of focus, discipline, harmony, and teamwork. Managers like Sam were looked upon to improve the capability of processes. For the most part, however, Sam's newly adopted modus operandi had been producing just the opposite.

At management's request, I had come to Titanium Enterprises to help the company take a new look at the effectiveness of the entire organization. Once there, the company asked me to have a talk with Sam, too. Listening to their assessment, I couldn't help wondering if I was hearing the whole story. There is often more to a case of employee dysfunction than meets the eye, with unresolved organizational issues responsible for more visible symptoms. I had discovered this time and again at other client companies, and I had a suspicion something similar was going on here at Titanium.

Titanium's top managers believed Sam's antagonistic behavior had become an obstacle to their goals. Yet no one inside the company seemed to be having any luck talking to him about it. Perhaps an objective outsider such as myself—one experienced in sorting through interpersonal as well as structural issues—could get through to Sam. I told top management that I would give it a try.

Later that day, I met with Sam. Unlike the monster he had been portrayed as being, I immediately found him courteous, reasonable, intelligent, and mature. If anything, he seemed both painstakingly aware of his accountabilities and of the objectives of the company. Sam was sincere in his desire to carry them out. But that, I was to find, was at the root of his undoing.

I asked Sam how he felt about his promotion to assistant superintendent. Although grateful for the chance to advance himself, he had actually applied for the superintendent's position (his manager's job), he told me, only to be turned down and given *this* position instead. Sam had really wanted that higher position and believed he could do well in it, even though it was one full level higher. So his first emotion in connection with his new job was frustration that management had not recognized his potential. And once he'd started this job, his frustration had grown worse.

Sam was right: He was clearly overqualified for this role. His level of "horsepower"—that is, his innate ability to handle complexity—indicated that he did, indeed, hold the current potential to function at a higher level on Titanium's corporate ladder than he was at now. A couple of Titanium's senior managers immediately concurred with this assessment. Despite the availability of straightforward systems for doing so, carefully assessing intellectual capacity when placing someone in a valuable role is something most companies unfortunately ignore. This frequently results in much time lost, many wasted resources, widespread dwindling morale, or worse.

Nonetheless, Sam's promotion was a step in the right direction. Why would such a turn of events account for Sam's newfound mean streak and dysfunctional behavior? Couldn't he do this job as well as possible while keeping alert to the chance to move up again? I probed on.

"They say my job is to get these 40-year-old machines running at 68-percent capacity," Sam told me, "and more if I can get them up there. But I've never been able to reach any level higher than 60 percent. No one else at Titanium has ever gotten capacity above 55 percent. And now that I'm in this job I can understand why. Most operators on the floor just won't follow my directions!"

Sam explained that it was his job to get at least two of the six machines on the shop floor running above 66-percent capacity every day if he could. But the machines' operators consistently resisted him on it. They refused to make the changes he requested. They claim this or that adjustment just couldn't be done and that the shift supervisor would never approve it.

"They're afraid that if something happened to a machine, if it broke down because it had been cranked up too high, they'll catch hell for it from their immediate supervisors," Sam elaborated. "I'm not their 'real' boss and they know it. Their real bosses are the shift supervisors who can dock their pay, suspend them, fire them, whatever. And they're so busy fighting fires around here, attending to other matters, they just dismiss me when I bring the problem to their attention. They say I should be able to handle it myself, that that's my job. Well, it is—except I can only do so much, especially when the operators know full well they don't actually report to me."

Sam was clearly grateful to have an opportunity to talk to someone—anyone—about his dilemma. Sam chuckled nervously as he thought about it some more. He recalled, "I tried to talk to them about it at first, but I never seemed to be getting anywhere. Their supervisors were always off handling some crisis, so they had no time for me anyway. And it was easier for them to just agree with the operators; they, too, were afraid of pushing the machines too hard."

Sam continued, "I began to realize the only thing I could really do was to make a fuss, to yell, or to carry on. Even Fred, my boss, was always too preoccupied with other things to go to bat for me. He seemed to be so busy with his own crises and compliance issues, forever buried in paperwork, that he just kept telling me, 'Handle it yourself.' I couldn't seem to get through to him. I was caught in a bind. Fred never saw my dilemma as ultimately his problem to solve.

"So I found that when I make plenty of noise, the operators would do what I said, at least for a little while. After a day or two, though, they always find a way to slip right back to running their machines the way they were doing before."

The problem was becoming clear. Sam had been given accountability for getting his area's machines operating at more than 60 percent but, along with it, he had not been given the commensurate authority. Only the operators' managers, the shift supervisors, could take measures to ensure that orders were carried out. However, because of their own preoccupations, they rarely took any steps to back Sam up. Even when they did, they never followed through with their people. Sam could do little else but advise and suggest. He had basically been left to figure ways to compensate for his lack of authority in whatever manner he could.

I had observed this dynamic too many times before, at too many companies. Each time, management's approval of it always seemed to make complete managerial sense to them. Its practice, however, epitomizes one of the great misconceptions about how to properly run a business—that is, assuming that throwing job performance expectations at employees without providing them commensurate authority to carry them out was an appropriate and effective way to get things done.

So I returned to top management and leveled with them. "Sam Travers operates the way he does because you've forced him to," I said. "You've created the monster who terrorizes your machine operators because he's been left no other choice. He carries out his duties the only way he knows how. Believe it or not, from his perspective, he's acting *responsibly.*"

Titanium's managers reacted with horror. Had they brought in the wrong consultant? "Our Sam Travers, responsible?" they grumbled. "The guy who rants, swears, and kicks things around? No way!"

Their confusion immediately reminded me of an occasion a few years earlier when I'd participated in a management conference in Rio de Janeiro. Though unfamiliar with Portuguese, I tried to listen to one of the speakers with two different earphones, one translating English in one of my ears and a second speaking Portuguese in the other. I was curious to see if I could pick up a bit of Portuguese this way.

I wasn't successful at learning much of the language, but I did notice that the words "responsibility" and "accountability" kept cropping up quite a lot in the English version. Yet every time the translation came through in Portuguese it was always the same word, "responsibilidad." I assumed that this must really mean "responsibility," so I wondered why the equivalent word for "accountability" was not coming through.

After this talk, I asked one of my Brazilian hosts about this. She looked dismayed. "Responsibility and accountability? The word in Portuguese for them both is responsibilidad," she said. "They do mean the same thing, do they not?"

I had an epiphany at that moment as I realized how so much of the world fails to appreciate the distinction. Responsibility and accountability, the same thing? In the United States, too, these words are often used interchangeably as well. Yet, the truth is very different. The two words have two very distinct meanings.

In the case of Titanium Enterprises, for example, Sam had been given accountability to carry out certain objectives, yet he had actually assumed a mantel of responsibility. By taking it upon himself to carry out company objectives any way he could, Sam compensated for a personal power vacuum created by the fact that he had not been given commensurate *authority* to back up his mandate. As such, his pride in wanting to do a good job, and his desperation to find a way to do so, really drove his responsible actions, dysfunctional as they seemed. Without proper authority, he could conceive of no other way to fulfill his accountabilities to his own boss or to upper management.

In light of its own ill-conceived management practices, Titanium Enterprises had failed to realize how lucky it was to have such a responsible-minded assistant superintendent. In the service of responsibility, Sam went so far as to play the role of an unpopular, unlikable troublemaker, a position that he confessed to me did not suit him. Yet, if that was what it would take to get those machines going full tilt, then that was exactly what he was willing to commit himself to do.

To continue the story, after discussing with Titanium's top management the ramifications of what they had been doing, things began to change. Top managers realized, for the first time, that their splitting up of the accountabilities of process, equipment, and people (assistant superintendents, shift supervisors) had resulted in no one manager being fully accountable for the operators getting the right results with the right process at the right machine. They also realized that too many accountabilities opposed each other. Sam's mandate to get the operators to run their machines at higher capacities, for example, conflicted with the shift supervisors' accountability to keep machines from overheating or breaking down.

The structure and authorities were changed to bring about alignment. The position of shift supervisor, accountable only for managing the machine operators, was eliminated. Top management appointed Sam, along with three other colleagues, to newly created positions called area managers. In these new first-line managerial positions, Sam and the other three area managers were given full 24/7 managerial authority over people, processes, and equipment within each machine area, so that they could manage and change machine processes however they deemed necessary.

The accountabilities were no longer divided. Managers were no longer working at odds. And Sam now had the authority he needed to fulfill his accountabilities.

As a result, all operators in his area, across all four shifts, began supporting Sam's plans. Complaints, once so prevalent, stopped immediately, as did Sam's aberrant behavior. The operators no longer felt threatened and Sam no longer needed to scold, intimidate, or scream at them.

Instead, Sam and the operators began engaging in productive context setting. He explained clearly to the operators his own accountabilities and thinking and the thinking from upper management, and the operators offered positive feedback and ideas of their own. All Titanium managers, at every level, received leadership training from The Levinson Institute, putting the final piece in place for a full accountability leadership system. Before long, when his own supervisor failed to master the requirements of his redefined role, Sam was promoted to the position he had wanted all along: superintendent.

In terms of quantitative results, machine capacity on the floor began significant upturn during all these changes. By the time Sam became superintendent, capacity was running consistently at roughly 75- to 80-percent capacity even from the toughest machine they referred to as the "Red Devil," unheard of before the reorganization. Steady momentum continued each and every day, far beyond what expectations at Titanium Enterprises had ever been. Where 60 percent had once seemed all but unattainable, 65 percent was now the bottom threshold.

Accountability leadership had leveraged, engaged, aligned, and developed its power once again!

Chapter 14
Chat with the Author

In preparation for this book, I sat down with noted management writer Tom Gorman to freewheel thoughts about LEAD principles and their implications for the future of business. This chapter offers an edited version of our discussion and takes up such topics as:

- Good vs. bad hierarchy.
- QQT/Rs.
- Linked chains of accountability.
- Why empowerment doesn't work.
- Elliott Jaques and role complexity.
- Harry Levinson and the psychological contract.
- HR fads.
- Alignment.
- Mentoring.

TG: Let's start with leveraging.

GK: The function of leadership is to leverage the full potential of all of the organization's resources to accomplish its mission in a way that the leader could not accomplish on his own. Accountability is one of the attributes of an effective managerial leadership system—one that influences the types of leverage required: positional [authority] together with the psychological [trust and credibility].

TG: What about the LEAD process? How does that connect to accountability per se?

GK: LEAD transcends accountability. Accountability is actually one of the subsets of LEAD. Remember, leadership of any sort—managerial, political, moral, religious—is about leveraging the potential of your people, your tools, your concepts, your ideas, to create something greater than the leader could do on his own or that the parts could do separately.

In managerial systems, leveraging is best accomplished by fully engaging the hearts and minds of your people. This requires attending to the psychological contract. It also requires aligning people's thinking, decisions, and actions, which involves context-setting, organizational alignment, getting process accountabilities clear—within an accountability framework—and developing the capabilities of all your resources, especially your human resources, to work at full potential.

So accountability really shows up as a subtext under the "A" in LEAD. It is leveraging the full potential of your resources, engaging the hearts and minds of your people, aligning thinking, decisions, and actions *within an accountability framework,* and developing the full potential of your people.

TG: Can you describe accountability leadership in a sentence or two?

GK: It's actually going to encompass several of the things. For example, you talk with any group about accountability and ask them what it is, and they'll say it's about who do you blame when things go wrong. You ask them how it feels and they'll say it doesn't feel good. You ask them if they welcome being accountable, and they'll say, "Under the present circumstances, no." So why has accountability gotten a bad rap?

It's because it has been invoked as a way for senior executives to get things done within a structure that doesn't support getting things done. Yet somehow [they believe] that by magically telling people "you're accountable," it *will* get it done. That's what accountability has come to mean, not what it really should mean.

TG: Which is?

GK: Which is the obligation—if we're talking about an employment organization— the obligation of the employee to deliver on all elements of the value that that person is being compensated for [delivering] in the role that he or she is in.

TG: Why doesn't this usually happen?

GK: It requires a rigor of thinking that most managers are either too lazy to engage in or haven't been given the tools with which to exercise it effectively or don't intrinsically value it. Most importantly, I believe it doesn't happen because people have moved too far away from common sense.

For example, you're a cog in a huge wheel or a cog in a huge set of wheels. You don't feel any responsibility for the money that's being spent on your subordinate, *and* you're not being held accountable for demonstrating the value that your resources are contributing to the organization. It is a whole lot easier to ignore it and to focus on just getting people "doing things" rather than holding them accountable for delivering on their commitments and delivering on the value over and above their commitments.

So accountability simply represents a mutually agreed-upon obligation based upon mutually agreed-upon commitments to exchange value.

TG: Shifting a bit, you have kind of knocked empowerment in your writings. But didn't that come about with the shift in the economy from physical work to mental work, and from where quality is easily quantifiable, such as products produced in a manufacturing environment, to less quantifiable results—work requiring much more, as you put it, judgment and creativity? They weren't empowering people just because they're humanists, they were businesspeople feeling that that was what they had to do in that kind of work environment. Even a customer service person needs to be empowered or she can't solve customers' problems. Right?

GK: I would challenge your assumptions about why that all came about. It didn't come about because of a shift from physical work to judgment work. Work has been judgment work for centuries. The shift came about because some companies were more effective in harnessing and leveraging judgment than others were. Older companies weren't able to compete by rigidly adhering to mechanistic tradition. So they, too, had to become more adaptive.

Then Jack Welch came along and said, "We're not going to accept functioning at 20 percent of our potential," and he started listening to his people, getting everyone to add his own value to the equation. But what some people didn't observe was that he also had no problem holding people accountable at the same time.

Instead, the rest of the world said, "Oh my God! Japan is beating our socks off, and GE is beating our socks off. What are they doing? Hey, they're getting people more involved. They must be empowering people." And so they looked only at one aspect of the behavior, not at the underlying shift in the successful organizations. The behavior was that people were now exercising more judgment. But in GE, people weren't empowered as such. They were given more authority *and* they were given it within an accountability framework.

TG: How did all the other companies react to that, specifically?

GK: Most companies now said, "You're all empowered. If you see something wrong, go and change it." The trouble was that when they saw something wrong, the involved process had not been capable of supporting the recommended change. So someone changed something and something got done but the action screwed up a larger process.

The issue of empowerment is "how much" power. Do I have the power to ignore my manager? Do I have the power to ignore the impact of a short cycle time? Do I have the power to increase our cost structure, so that we get more sales but no profit? The point is that it's abdication, the way that empowerment has been applied in our organizations. "We don't know what to tell you to do, so go ahead and use your judgment." And then the problem shifts and becomes even worse. "I wash my hands of it. You fix it."

What you end up with is a lot of people who've been frustrated by bad organizations and they're now uncorked and saying, "Great!" And you'll start seeing improved productivity in their area, but it will *always* be at the expense of the rest of the organization.

Managerial leadership systems are, by definition, distributed decision-making hierarchies. And when you distribute and delegate the authority to make decisions, that's where the real power is. But if you anoint everyone with the power to do whatever makes sense to them, then everybody's own interpretation of what makes sense reigns supreme. And you find yourself with this chaotic ripple effect in which everything cancels everything else out.

The intention behind empowerment—let's break people free from the shackles of a rigid, unadaptive, uncommunicative bureaucracy—was a great idea. But the intention without the substance behind it is often worse than just the intention. It can be such a nightmare!

TG: What about hierarchy and good and bad hierarchy?

GK: Hierarchy is equated with bureaucracy in most people's minds, so when they hear the word they react as they do when they hear accountability. It conjures up rigidity, red tape, too many levels, a need for constant permission and approvals for every move, second-guessing of decisions, and extreme risk-aversion.

To me hierarchy is neither good nor bad intrinsically. Hierarchy is a fact of life. Bones break, but that doesn't mean they are bad. Hierarchy is an intrinsic property of managerial systems. Managerial systems are, by their very nature, accountability hierarchies. The only reason that the shareholders would trust their board of directors to delegate to a CEO authority over their resources is that the shareholders hold the board accountable for the CEO's output. The only reason that the board would trust the CEO to delegate some of those resources to the EVP is that they hold the CEO accountable for the EVP's output. So hierarchy is an intrinsic property of an accountability managerial system.

At the same time, one of Elliott Jaques's discoveries was that when you look through the organization, there are other kinds of hierarchies as well *and* there are naturally distinct levels of complexity. So it's not only an accountability hierarchy. It's also a distributed decision-making hierarchy and a complexity/ judgment hierarchy.

TG: What do you mean by complexity/judgment?

GK: When you look at the nature of work, spanning vertically from the bottom to the top of the organization, the work increases not only in degrees of complexity as you move up the organization; the work literally changes the nature of complexity periodically. And there are naturally occurring levels of complexity, which is another form of hierarchy. Jaques called it strata, like geologists talk about it. He referred to his system as Stratified Systems Theory.

So hierarchy is intrinsically neither good nor bad. Bad hierarchy, which is what we equate with bureaucracy, is when we have too many levels and when we have managers who are not adding value. Bad hierarchy is when we have abdication, on the one hand, where managers are not clear about accountabilities. Or, on the other, it is when managers tell people that they're accountable but then don't give them the decision-making authority to meet their accountabilities. Bad hierarchy is when managers basically don't give people any authority and the managers themselves make all the decisions. That's command and control.

Good hierarchy exists in managerial systems when the levels are properly defined and the roles are properly established. They are populated by people whose capabilities are well matched to their roles. They are led by managers who give them the level of authority necessary to make the decisions they need. That's not empowerment. That is effective, creativity-releasing hierarchy. So that's what I mean by good hierarchy.

TG: Can you point to anybody doing it right and doing it wrong?

GK: Just go to the annual *BusinessWeek* or *Fortune* top 1,000 in terms of EBITDA (earnings before interest, taxes, depreciation, and amortization) and I guarantee you that those in the top 200 are doing it more right and those in the bottom 200 are doing it real bad.

TG: Watch out. They're ranked by revenue.

GK: They also rank them by EBITDA. Two or three years ago GM was 998th in EBITDA, and they had bad hierarchy. They had 13 levels and they only need eight.

TG: You can be that precise?

GK: That's the point. There is a science that Jaques discovered about the elements of good hierarchy. Ford, until two or three years ago, was 995th and they had 12 levels and now they're starting to pare them out, whereas Chrysler, which was around 250th before the Daimler acquisition, got rid of those levels

15 years ago because Lee Iaccoca realized the company couldn't afford them. They made a virtue out of necessity. They established full P&L-account business units. Most of Ford is still only one P&L-account business unit headed up by the corporate CEO, Jacques Nasser.

So there are all kinds of examples. There are some that have been consistently effective. For instance, GE and 3M—they have always understood intuitively the importance of getting the right functional alignment, getting business-unit size right, giving the heads of those business units sufficient authority to make decisions. In the pharmaceutical industry, Johnson & Johnson has always been known as the least centralized. People say they are decentralized and very successful. My point is that they're not decentralized; they're properly structured and properly led.

TG: So it's not about whether you're centralized or decentralized. It's about whether you're properly or improperly structured.

GK: You bet.

TG: QQT/R—what about that? Why is that such a powerful way to think about assignments?

GK: If you ask most employees how clear their managers are with them as to what they are accountable for getting work done, most of them will say, "Not very."

TG: Even in manufacturing environments, with production quotas and so on?

GK: They'll always talk about results or limits or maybe a specific output, but not the kinds of assignments that are necessary to yield those results. So in a manufacturing environment you can say to someone, "I want you to improve the output by 20 percent." But if you're not real clear with them about at what cost and how much, quality can suffer.

If you think about it, the elements of a QQT/R are interdependent variables. If you start falling behind on one, you can adjust the others and make up for it. And if you're going to have any control over the system, managers and subordinates have to be bound together by clearly articulated obligations.

Now the subordinate is obligated to deliver the QQ by T and the manager is obligated to deliver the R. What often happens in companies is that the manager will get stretch commitments from a subordinate, which aren't real in the first place. Then, in the course of the year, she finds that she can't deliver on the resources but still expects her subordinate to deliver the Q and Q. That's where people feel as though they've been snookered.

So, QQT/R is a very powerful and very rational concept to keep everyone honest. People in project management use it all the time.

TG: Its power lies in its precision, correct?

GK: The power lies in the *result* of the precision, which is that I now know exactly what it is my boss means for me to deliver. And I won't get hit over the head the way I used to when I delivered on what I thought it was and it turned out to be different from what he wanted. So yes, the precision gets it there, but the point is that the QQT/R enables managers to define their intentions more *precisely.*

TG: What do you mean about QQT/Rs and the metaphor of linked chains of accountability?

GK: The usual reflex to say that hierarchy, aka bureaucracy, is bad translates into a reference to command and control and to implicitly invoke a gear mechanism. And if you think about the relationship between the top gear and a gear five gears [or levels] down, the amount of discretion that any gear below the top has for independently exercising judgment is nil. And a little bit of movement from the top [large] gear causes the bottom gears to go into a rapid whirling in circles.

TG: Happens all the time.

GK: This gear image does address the legitimate need for control when you're trying to have an orchestrated execution of strategy. But it leaves no room for judgment, which is what we're trying to harness in getting the execution of strategy. The other extreme is empowerment, in which we have everyone thinking but no one accountable or in control. The image here is Brownian movement.

Now, the linked chain metaphor gets closer to what we're trying to convey. The managerial leadership system must optimally deploy the judgment of everyone in the organization. But it does not release the CEO from accountability for what they all do. So they are all bound by this chain, which is essentially held together by the QQT/Rs—the fixed commitments—and by the process limitations and policy limitations. What you want is for people to have some room for movement. You want them to have some freedom to exercise judgment and discretion *within the limits* that are necessary to bring the whole thing together. The QQT/Rs become the connector links that hold this whole accountable judgment system together.

Actually, the linked-chain metaphor works to a modest degree, but one limitation is that it implies that this system is only vertical. In most organizations, most of the work flows horizontally. My wife came up with the metaphor of a knitted sweater. If you snip one link, nothing will happen. If the organization is in a static, uncompetitive environment in which all you need to do is what you've always done, no problem. But if you're in a dynamic, changing environment that requires every link to exercise new kinds of judgment, watch out! When you start to stretch that sweater, it will begin to unravel.

And that's what happens in empowered organizations in a rapidly dynamic environment. Some people even try to tout the value of it. Tom Peters does so with chaos theory, leading by chaos.

TG: Right, but in earlier books he had the business of the simultaneously tight and loose management: being tight about expectations but loose in allowing people to use their judgment in how to reach those expectations.

GK: When he says that, I'm fine. Unfortunately, to most people empowerment means do whatever you think is right.

TG: To get the result required by the job.

GK: The big problem is that most employees don't have their outputs well defined. So it comes across as "do whatever you need for your unit to achieve its output," and what you end up with for the entire process is a crapshoot.

TG: Or it's even looser. Do whatever you need to do to realize the company vision or the mission statement that is over there hanging on the wall of the cafeteria. When some people take that seriously you get some really wild-horse behavior.

GK: Years ago I saw old *The New Yorker* cartoon in which two theoretical physicists were at the blackboard with all of these arcane symbols and then in the middle it says, "And then a great miracle occurs." The first scientist says to the second one, "I think you need to tighten the equation up in the middle." That's what I believe empowerment is: good intentions. But the point is how do you get the whole to come together?

TG: What are the most common mistakes managers make in this broad area of accountability? We've more or less covered a number of them already: lack of clarity, not knowing the expectations yourself, under-resourcing, not making QQT/Rs clear....

GK: Basically it's lack of clarity about what someone is accountable for doing— the QQT/R. It's also lack of clarity about the context—why and how it fits in. People are flying blind if they don't know the why and the how of their managers' thinking even if they do know the what. What they end up doing is spending lots of time trying to figure out a solution to the wrong problem.

Another is lack of alignment about what you say I'm accountable for and what I really have the authority to accomplish. That's a *huge* disconnect. And there is usually the lack of an overarching framework that would clarify for people on how they should go about resolving differences between them.

TG: Structural or strategic?

GK: The lack of framework exists for several reasons, sometimes structural, sometimes a failure to articulate strategy. Most often it is a failure to translate strategy into actionable items. Most business opportunities are lost by organizations when they have many people operating in a vacuum, doing their own thing. When there are obstacles or opportunities in front of people that require them to make adjustments in relationship to each other, a lack of encompassing framework prevents them from maximizing or optimizing the whole organization's results. Even when you have people who want to do the right thing, the best they come up with is a negotiated compromise that they can all live with. That's not good enough.

In fact, in these big matrix organizations, Ford and GM, they go out and hire negotiation trainers to teach people on staff how to negotiate with one another how to compromise. How sad!

What you want is not people to negotiate that solution they can all live with, but rather to come up with the solution that best supports the business's ultimate goal, even if it makes some of their jobs more difficult. People can't do that in a vacuum. It's the accountability of management at each level to define the framework within which the subordinates must operate—not all elements of every decision, but the principles and priorities that they need to reconcile when they come up with an approach in common.

TG: Now, why don't all managers do that? And that gets to your point.

GK: One reason they don't is if the *strategy* isn't clear in the first place. At the other extreme is the large number of matrix organizations for any people who need to work together from disparate parts of the organization—people whose first crossover doesn't come together until five levels up. In that situation, there's no way that the common manager could construct a meaningful umbrella or decision-making framework to problems so far removed. What you get are the generic mission statements you find hanging on the cafeteria wall. And that's a *structural* problem.

When you have people who need to be working intimately together to deliver the goods, and you have a highly functional organization—that is, one organized strictly along functional lines or with lots of departments that are not tied together closely enough—you have created the infamous silo effect. Everyone is operating inside separate, isolated silos. The attempt to resolve this is usually via cross-functional working or output teams. As you saw in Chapter 7, this creates another whole set of problems.

When you get right down to it, though, the real reason managers don't do it is that they're too lazy. Henry Ford said 100 years ago, "Thinking is the hardest work there is, which is why so few managers engage in it." That rings true today.

TG: You have mentioned before that the work of Elliott Jaques has been central to the development of LEAD principles.

GK: At the core of a managerial leadership system lies an employment organization fueled by people's judgment. We're not employing knowledge, skill, or commitment. We're employing people applying their judgment *with* knowledge, skill, and commitment. But the reason we're employing their judgment is to solve problems necessary for the organization to create the value that it has promised to create. So that's the essence of what we're really employing: judgment. And by judgment I mean the work of solving the problems necessary to achieve goals.

Judgment is enhanced by knowledge. And the degree to which this judgment and knowledge are effectively applied is enhanced to the degree to which people are committed and mature. But in the end, we're primarily employing judgment.

Elliott discovered some critical properties of judgment and complexity. So there are two things valuable to understand in the beginning, because then everything else makes a lot more sense.

First, Elliott discovered the essence of what distinguishes smaller roles from bigger roles. Bigger roles are more complex. That's the essential difference. It's not that you can identify a particular thing that's more complex; it's *all* of the work. Elliott discovered a way of measuring complexity called time-span. It has to do with the time horizon that you have to consider in your job.

Once he had this way of measuring complexity, he then made an important discovery: There are different true levels of complexity in organizations and everyone recognizes intuitively that they are there.

So when you have what some people call relatively unskilled and semi-skilled and skilled operators, they're all at the same level. The terms unskilled, semi-skilled, and skilled have no real meaning.

When you go to the next true level, whether it's a supervisor of those folks or an entry-level professional of some sort, they may be dealing with different tasks, but they, too, are all on the same level of complexity. Then you go up and up the ladder, and you're dealing progressively with more different types of complexity. At the same time, we find that people at different levels require different forms of information. And we can identify and describe those as well.

It took Elliott almost 40 years to figure out what those different levels are doing in every single leadership system he investigated in more than 20 countries and more than 19 different industries. What are they doing there? Where is it written that one should never have more than eight levels in our super-corporations? Why not? He found these discontinuous levels in all human-employment-managerial systems. Elliott noticed that the one thing the systems all have in common is they are all trying to figure out how to organize and deploy people. Also, he found that managers have an intuitive recognition that people differ in the way they handle various kinds of complexity.

What we now know, too, from his research, is that people exist on a continuum, from less sharp to more sharp to very sharp. You can substitute clever, bright, smart, creative, and so forth, for "sharp."

TG: We're getting into judgment now?

GK: We're moving from complexity to judgment. Complexity refers to the type of work that needs to be done. Judgment is the type of mental process necessary to do the work. And Elliott discovered that although human beings do exist on a continuum of greater or lesser degrees of judgment—that is, capacity to handle complexity—at a certain point, when people mature to the next increment of judgment, they actually change the *kind* of judgment they're capable of.

TG: Qualitatively?

GK: Qualitatively. It's not just quantitatively higher. They literally start to think differently.

TG: For example?

GK: Okay. A policeman only needs to be able to apply a procedure when finding a scene of the crime. He knows what kind of evidence to collect, how to collect it properly, and how to put it together. But he isn't expected to make the judgment that a detective does, which is to piece the evidence together and find a pattern. There is a step change.

And the detective isn't expected to understand how to improve a technical process doing analysis. That level of complexity requires the next level of judgment.

TG: Who is that, the forensic guy? I thought you were going to go up to the prosecutor, the DA.

GK: I guess I could do that. But this is the point: What Elliott reasoned and was able to observe in people engaged in debate or discussion was that we recognize intuitively, within minutes, people who differ in mental capacity. And it's not by listening to what they say, but *how* they construct their arguments. It's restating Descartes: "I link, therefore I am!" It's the particular links that people are able to make. And each connection is at right angles to the one below it. That's what managers do to add value when their roles are situated one level above their subordinates. They elevate their subordinates by helping them to understand their work from the manager's level of complexity.

TG: I see.

GK: This becomes the starting point in moving from structure to people. It's here that we have the greatest piece of confirmed scientific evidence. If we can accurately measure the size of the role that we want, and we are confident that we can accurately judge the type of mental process a person has the current ability to exercise, then we know whether that person has the *potential* to be effective in that role.

Whether he will actually perform well will also depend on whether he knows enough, he's skilled enough, he cares enough, and he's mature enough. But if you don't have the raw ability to handle the complexity required by the role, you're going to whittle the role down to the size that you can handle. And that's what's happened to IBM under John Ackers, GM under Robert Stempel—organization after organization, it's Archimedes' principle in reverse, as Elliott used to put it. The capability of the entire organization will rise and fall with the capability of the senior executive officer. The capability of any function will rise and fall with the capability of its senior executive.

You might have someone who is innately quite capable. But that individual might not be able to manage his way out of a paper bag. So the raw capability is a necessary, but not a sufficient, condition.

So to apply LEAD to exercise leverage, we have to understand that we employ people for their judgment. We need to understand the nature of judgment in relation to the complexity of work. When we understand that, then we can start to make sense out of the rest of the LEAD elements and their application.

So that's one key area.

TG: What's the next?

GK: The second key area of understanding is that you are employing human beings with judgment—not robots. You're employing human beings, who are intentional creatures. People must first commit themselves to apply their judgment, to acquire the skills and knowledge necessary to be effective, and to work within the constraints of an accountability system—if you are to leverage their potential.

TG: Can we talk about the psychological contract? One of the things that struck me is that you rightly point out that people will commit to the extent that they see evidence that the organization is reciprocally committed to them.

GK: Harry Levinson, who coined the term "psychological contract," developed lenses necessary to understand how to engage employee commitment. Harry basically said that the starting point of the psychological contract, the degree to which there is affinity and mutual passion, is whether or not people have a sense of common purpose or common value. "If we don't have enough interest in common," he claimed, "we may be cordial, but we won't be passionate." Common purpose is the glue that binds people together in a relationship.

Having a common purpose permits the basis for a relationship, but it doesn't ensure the health of the relationship. And here Harry talks about three dimensions that determine the distance between people in the relationship. The first is the degree to which each employee or manager respects the other's legitimate need for control. This includes the degree to which employees respect the organization's need to define their accountabilities and to define its strategy. And, on the other side, it explores the degree to which the organization respects that people must be given the authority to deliver on their accountabilities and that they need to have input into and, to some degree, control over their careers. So on the one hand, there is this need for control.

Second, he described mutual needs of affection or positive regard. Employees need to be recognized and appreciated. And the company needs its people to enthusiastically work together to support its goal.

Harry explained that there must be a reciprocal understanding of, and respect for, each other's need for privacy. I have to have a life of my own outside the company. And the company, too, needs to retain the right to hold tight its secrets and keep its skeletons locked in a closet.

And finally, the third dimension is the degree to which people are committed to supporting the legitimate needs of others during times of change. The employee must understand that her organization has to adapt to a constantly changing environment. She can't expect her employer to simply maintain the status quo and support her comfort level. It is the organization's proper role, Harry said, to continually adapt and evolve in relationship to the requirements of the environment, for the purpose of supporting both the shareholders and the firm's employees.

At the same time, there needs to be an understanding that, as the organization changes and expects its people to change, it has a reciprocal obligation to support its employees in helping them to successfully get through the change.

So it's about balancing the tensions arising from the mutual dependence, distance, and the change. Arthur Schopenhauer, the nineteenth-century philosopher, talked about two porcupines trying to huddle together to keep warm in the winter, close enough so that they can experience warmth, but not close enough for them to stick each other.

Harry Levinson's genius was in identifying how these dimensions take on a different form or style in different organizations. Yet there are universal human needs that will determine the overall level of trust and commitment employees have. They are: a safe and healthy work environment; meaningful, purposeful work; challenging work; working conditions that allow one to be successful; the commitment to develop people to work at their full potential; recognition and compensation; and a fair, just, and respectful working environment. In addition, people need to see evidence that their input is not only solicited and valued but that it makes a difference—that it is incorporated in the organization's thinking and actions.

TG: Input into their daily job responsibilities or ideas for improvement?

GK: Input into everything. Helping managers think through what the work is, around their own accountabilities, around improvement. People need to see that they are able to contribute to the larger whole not just in doing what they are told to do but in helping to formulate what the organization does and should do. There is also the whole notion about the degree to which managers include them in the thinking of the organization and in their own thinking.

Someone pointed out to me only recently that people also must believe their organization is fully committed to its own healthy perpetuation, not just to expedient decisions. Because if I'm going to invest my career in this or that organization, I don't want to do it if the organization might self-destruct midway through my career.

All of these are the areas of tangible, testable commitment on the part of the organization that demonstrates to the employee its commitment to help the employee to be successful.

TG: What would you say to the charge that that's either idealistic or a throwback to the mid-1950s? When it comes to commitment to employees, many organizations do walk the walk as well as talk the talk. But many others are almost nakedly frank about, "You'll be here for maybe three years. But you'll learn a lot and then move on."

GK: If the two questions are, "Are there organizations that have adopted that posture and are some of them successful in the near term?" the answer to both is yes. But the thing that you also hear from these organizations is that when they have turnovers of 30 to 40 percent a year, the cost to the organization is incredible. In particular, the drain, the distraction, the lack of focus, and the demoralization that results from the turnover that occurs. The economic cost of recruitment and more. It can take a year or 18 months to get someone up to speed in an organization. If he's gone a year and a half after that, you really haven't gotten much of a return on your initial investment.

Yet you hear so much talk these days in the HR workshops (all of these talent retention and compensation workshops) that you have to treat these folks as if they're carrying their "brain portfolios" with them. So the current thinking seems to be to squeeze as much juice as you can out of them and then let them move on.

TG: I'm surprised that the HR people are that resigned.

GK: Oh, they are! The fact is that, just as the biotech and the high-tech and the dotcom bubbles have been bursting, this is going to burst, too. Many organizations are not fully committed to developing mature, successful psychological contracts with their people. They are not able to build the people they need from within—as well as being able to attract people from outside. They are destined for a short half-life, no question in my mind. They will just not be able to sustain themselves.

TG: What you're saying is counter-current or counter-trend, because most people are expecting six or seven careers in this lifetime, that it's all about portable skills and all of that. But what you're saying is also very sensible for companies to hear because we're currently in the midst of such a raging talent shortage. And when there's a talent shortage, there are only two good options: grow it here or shut your doors. And that's all, right?

GK: Exactly. Recently, I had a visit from a senior HR executive from India, here on an Eisenhower fellowship. He's 35 years old, and he has two Ph.D.s. He's a brilliant man. It was a delight to spend time with him. His company employs 100,000 people.

Three days earlier he had attended a Society of Human Resource Management conference on retention in the world of work. And what they were saying was, "Don't worry about an internal compensation system. Just pay top dollar. It's all market value. Hold them while you can. Drive them while you can. Handcuff them."

This clever executive saw everyone nodding his or her heads and he asked himself, "What world am I in?" When he said that to me, I instantly replied, "You're in the world of American fads, of simplistic, instant-gratification responses. Because the demand for more complexity overwhelms people, they, instead, search for quick-fix easy answers."

TG: Could we talk about alignment? Alignment with the manager's thinking, the CEO's thinking, co-workers' thinking.

GK: For me alignment can be found on every level. It's alignment of judgment, alignment of values, alignment of the team, and it's alignment of the processes, alignment of the structure. It's all alignment, and that's why we talk about an integrated LEAD system.

For me the starting point of alignment is aligning accountability with authority. Next is aligning judgment of the different parts with a common perspective. You can subsume all of structure and process by saying align accountability with authority. Then you have to have the judgment alignment, which is setting context. Those are the two principal pieces.

Accountability without authority is fantasy and responsibility and stress. Authority without accountability is fantasy and entitlement and self-absorption.

TG: You've talked about a decision-making framework for finding optimal solutions. What determines the size of that decision-making umbrella? Is it the level of complexity or the manager's role or what?

GK: Let me answer that first by saying that I believe managers are the most narcissistic creatures on earth because they all believe their people should be able to read their minds. "Why did you to that?" a manager will ask. The employee will say, "Because that's what you told me to," or "you didn't tell me anything." "Well," the managers say, "that's not what I meant." "Well, how could I know?" comes the subordinate's response.

Managers assume that because *they've* thought it through that everyone else understands it. That's their first mistake. The second thing that's important to understand is that no human being is ever fully aware of *why* he has come to a particular decision. You can be aware of the things you considered in coming to the decision, but you can't understand the thousands of different experiences that resulted in the actual decision.

So managers have a problem. If they want their subordinates working together, coming together to make adjustments that will best support the manager's intention, how must they convey their thinking so their people can think on their behalf without their manager actually being there?

TG: Isn't the answer plain old communication?

GK: Yes, the answer *is* communication. But it is a very disciplined, structured type of communication. It's very difficult for a manager to just walk into a room and say, "Let me explain to you my entire logic so that you can act to replicate it." Instead, a manager needs to say, "Here's what I've come up with, and why, as best as I can reconstruct my thinking. These are the principles that went into it. Now I need each of you to feed back what you heard me say in your own words, so I can be sure that what you understood is what I meant. And I also need you to do that so that I can further understand whether you have a different view of it than I do. Because at the end of this context-setting conversation, I need for us together to understand and improve upon my reasoning process better than I understood it before we started."

That's the starting point for setting context effectively. I'm expecting, after having set the context with all of my reports, that they will further set context with each of *their* reports. And their context will include mine.

TG: And that's the mechanism you were referring to?

GK: Yes. Keep in mind that this works for managers of any three-level unit. So it might start with the superintendent and his supervisors and then be translated next to the machine operators. Or it might be the plant manager and his superintendent and his supervisors. Or it might be the division head and his plant manager and his superintendent. Any manager of a three-level unit, I believe, *must* construct a decision-making framework [a detailed extension of context] at the level of concreteness or abstraction that is appropriate to the bottom level.

TG: That abstraction can kill you.

GK: That's why I say at the appropriate level. So the superintendent will sit down with the supervisors and say, "On the night shift when the operators are here without any supervisors, these are the kind of things that could go on. Let's make sure we've covered the universe of likely things. We cannot consider every contingency, but if this kind of thing happens, these are the two or three options, therefore, and this is how we would think about them." So you construct it with the appropriate language, of course. It becomes more concrete at each lower level and more abstract at each higher level in the organization. But it's still the same concept and the same construct.

TG: Let's turn to development. What's most important to know here?

GK: The important part about the D in LEAD is that, because we're dealing with an accountability hierarchy, accountability includes not only delivering outputs, but also the stewardship of the resources delegated to deliver on those outputs. The stewardship of resources is not just applicable to processes and technology, but also to people. People have to be developed, continuously improved, just like any other resource.

The way a CEO meets his accountability for the development of the entire talent pool is by holding individual subordinates accountable for developing *their* subordinates in role. The CEO then reaches down and supports his subordinates-once-removed in their career development. In turn, the CEO's immediate subordinate develops that same subordinate [his immediate subordinate] in role and then reaches down another level and develops his skip-level subordinate in his career.

TG: In mentoring situations.

GK: Right. Mentoring is always two levels down; coaching is the immediate level down.

So it seems to me that the main thing to establish is that, although everyone speaks to development as a good thing—think apple pie and motherhood—it's the accountability for development that matters! What's key here is how is the CEO going to deliver on her accountability for enhancing the effectiveness of the talent pool? The answer can only be by holding each subordinate accountable for the stewardship of her next two levels of subordinates and cascading that down the entire system.

TG: You use the word "potential" a lot, and I think it's a popular word with executive-development professionals.

GK: When you think about it, high potential is simply an opportunity. It's not worth anything if it doesn't deliver.

TG: Right. And I think that's why it's suspect.

GK: My point is this: An immediate manager has to be accountable for delivering greater performance from subordinates. A skip-level manager has to identify how much more potential an individual two levels down has to handle a bigger role. And what can he or she do to qualify for a bigger role today? And how much potential does that person have to move up over his or her career? And how can the organization begin to develop the skip-level subordinate's experience and knowledge base so he can qualify for bigger roles as his potential or horsepower matures?

TG: And is realized.

GK: Well, it's more than that. It's about how do we *help* people realize their potential. See, that D in LEAD has two components. It's coaching by the immediate manager to enhance effectiveness—that is, performance in role. And it's mentoring by the skip-level manager to help the same individual acquire the additional qualifications to handle bigger roles as his career progresses.

TG: And the skip-level manager can do this without stepping on the toes of or alienating the manager below him?

GK: It requires sound communication, orchestration, and basic ground rules. The most important ground rule is that the employee cannot use the mentoring as a session to complain about his boss to his boss's boss. And it cannot be used by the skip-level manager to spy on his subordinate manager. It must be clear that this mechanism is for a very different purpose: for development and for the reinforcement of the company's commitment to that employee's development.

   In addition, the skip-level manager and the immediate manager have to communicate with each other effectively so the mentor can have a clear picture of the employee's demonstrated commitment and maturity. The mentor can then reinforce the manager's coaching by saying, "You've got the potential today to handle a bigger role, but you're not even cutting it very well in the role you're in. For me to invest the company's time and energies in developing you for a future role, we need to see more evidence of your commitment to fulfill your potential in the role you're already in."

So they must work as a tag team.

TG: That's excellent. It's also the first time I've heard a cogent explanation of mentoring. Elsewhere it's always this vague business of a guy who likes you...

GK: And takes you under his wing.

TG: Right.

GK: I can't tell you the millions of dollars that big companies—Lilly, Merck, others—are investing in mentoring programs. They go out to retreats. They talk. And whatever. It is terribly inefficient and ultimately unsuccessful because it is neither systematic nor accountable.

To succeed, mentoring and coaching are hard work. When successfully implemented, it is gratifying for everyone involved. It's mature work. It's intimate. But it ain't personal!

Bibliography

Brown, Wilfred and Elliott Jaques. *Glacier Project Papers.* London: Heinemann, 1965. Reprinted Gloucester, Mass.: Cason Hall Publishers, 1998.

Jaques, Elliott. *Equitable Payment,* 1961. Reprinted Gloucester, Mass.: Cason Hall Publishers, 1998.

Jaques, Elliott. *A General Theory of Bureaucracy.* London: Heinemann, 1976. Reprinted London: Greg Revivals, 1993.

Jaques, Elliott. *Measurement of Responsibility,* 1956. Reprinted Gloucester, Mass.: Cason Hall Publishers, 1998.

Jaques, Elliott. *Progression Handbook,* 1968. Reprinted Gloucester, Mass.: Cason Hall Publishers, 1998.

Jaques, Elliott. *Requisite Organization.* Gloucester, Mass.: Cason Hall Publishers, 1989 and 1996.

Jaques, Elliott and Kathryn Cason. *Human Capability.* Gloucester, Mass.: Cason Hall Publishers, 1994.

Kraines, Gerald A. "Essential Organization Imperatives." Cambridge, Mass.: The Levinson Institute, 1994.

Kraines, Gerald A. "Hierarchy's Bad Rap." *Journal of Business Strategy.* July–August 1996.

Levinson, Harry. *The Great Jackass Fallacy.* Cambridge, Mass.: Harvard University Press, 1973.

Levinson, Harry (with Charlton R. Price, Kenneth J. Munden, Harold J. Mandl, Charles M. Solley). *Men, Management, and Mental Health.* Cambridge, Mass.: Harvard University Press, 1962.

Levinson, Harry. *Ready, Fire, Aim: Avoiding Management by Impulse.* Cambridge, Mass.: The Levinson Institute, 1986.

Index

Potential
  and performance, 87-88
  as the capacity to handle
    complexity, 145
Potential, maturation of, 145-146
Predictable patterns of progression,
  91
Prescribing, 126
Process teams, 102
Proper alignment, 74
Psychological contract, 31, 60
  accountability framework and the,
    63-64
  common purpose and the, 61
  healthy distance and the, 61
  mutual commitment and the, 62-63
  outlines of the, 61-63
  negotiating a healthy, 35-36

Q

QQT/R, 18-21
  and the psychological contract, 37
  construction, 20
  definition, 83
QQT/Rs, 61, 171
QQT/Rs and
  mental capacity, 46
  personal value, 69
  role complexity, 47
Quest for responsibility, the, 180-183

R

Reach and employees, 17
Recommending as informing
accountability, 122
Recovery as third phase of critical
  change, 160-161

Relative accountabilities, 17-18, 33,
  88-89
Reorganization as fourth phase of
critical change, 161
Resisting context setting, 80
Role complexity,
  levels of, 134
  QQT/Rs and, 47

S

Self-directed teams, 102
Setting context, 35, 38
Six core accountabilities, 21
  at work, 21-22
Stewardship
  and employees, 17
  functions, 138
Strategic alignment's second coming,
  132-133
Study-recommendation-improvement
  team, the, 105-106
System stewardship, 134-135
Systems gone awry, 14-15

T

Team pitfalls, 110
Team-Accountability Myth, The,
  102-104
Teams and the search for
  accountability, 101-113
Teams, types of, 105-107
Teamwork and employees, 17
Teamworking context, 83
"Teamworking" meetings, 107
Three-level processes, 134
Titanium Enterprises, 187-192

About the Author

Gerald A. Kraines, M.D., is president and CEO of The Levinson Institute, a Boston-based leadership-development firm founded in 1968. The mission of the Institute is to advance the practice of leadership, improve the effectiveness of business organizations, and create the conditions necessary for all employees to realize their full potential. The Levinson Institute accomplishes this through seminars, consultation, publications, and research.

Dr. Kraines has consulted with scores of private and public organizations around the world, helping executives create leadership systems that yield real gains in productivity and long-term profitability. His parallel mission, from a public health perspective, is to help society create lasting constructive social institutions that promote human productivity and contribute to the general elevation of human dignity and pride. As a social scientist, Dr. Kraines strongly believes in promoting sound knowledge and common sense in companies. As a psychiatrist, he believes leaders must engage the hearts and elevate the minds of all people.